Dedicating Heart and Mind to God

Dedicating Heart and Mind to God

A Devotional from Corban University

Sheldon C. Nord, Ph.D.

This is a gift from Corban University—
something that will encourage and bless you
today and over the next few days and weeks.

It is an honor and privilege to work
alongside you in accomplishing God's
kingdom work in the many places
to which He has called us.

Soli Deo Gloria,

Sheldon C. Nord

Dedicating Heart and Mind to God:
A Devotional from Corban University

You can write to the author today at
president@corban.edu.

Picking Up the Pieces

Sheldon C. Nord, President
Corban University

Today's Reading: Psalm 147:3, 6, 11, 13

Today's Key Verse: "He heals the brokenhearted and binds up their wounds" (Psalm 147:3 NKJV).

Today's Insights: No one likes broken pieces. By their very nature, they imply that something is wrong. "Broken" is the opposite of "whole." Pieces of something that was once whole indicate that something disruptive happened, that harm was caused, and damage was done. And all of that points to pain.

Our theme at Corban University during the 2014-15 academic year was "Picking Up the Pieces." You might think that sounds incredibly dismal and wonder, "Why would a Christian university ever want a theme like that?"

It's a legitimate question. The theme is actually derived from our adoption of the four pillars of a biblical worldview: Authority/Truth, Creation, Fall, Redemption. This past year, we focused on the Fall and how that shapes our

3

understanding of the world. Perhaps you also experience seasons of "Picking Up the Pieces" in your businesses or in your family life.

We see the ramifications of the Fall every day—on the news, out and about, and in our own hearts. It's ugly, and it's everywhere. "It" is, of course, our sin.

But while our sin "so easily entangles" (Hebrews 12:1), and those broken pieces so mercilessly draw blood, **we have hope.** Our theme was actually grounded in Psalm 147:3, today's key verse, which again says: "He heals the brokenhearted and binds up their wounds."

Therein we see that the emphasis is actually not on our brokenness, but on the Healer of our brokenness. Jesus is the only one who can ever redeem a million shattered pieces. This is truth. This is our hope.

I told our students (and I encourage you to reflect on your own past year):

"I don't pretend to know what you personally experienced this past year. Perhaps it was a year you would classify as 'good.' And that is a blessing. Maybe you are delighting in new relationships built, classes you excelled in, or success you found on the athletic field or as a musician or thespian. My hope is that you made memories you will cherish for a lifetime.

4

"But I also know that life is hard—that you might look back on the school year and indeed feel broken. College is demanding, and Corban is particularly so because the goal for personal growth doesn't start and stop in the classroom. We want every student to be pushed mentally, physically, socially, and spiritually. So, 'broken' might just be your word of choice for this past school year.

"Just don't stop there, cut by the sharp pieces and overwhelmed by the Fall. We must take the pieces to our Healer, the Binder of our wounds, and ask Him to do the impossible. Only He can make us whole again. Only He can masterfully make beauty from rubble."

In coming days, as you read this devotional and are refreshed and renewed, I urge you to take your pieces to our Healer.

Keep Your Walk Simple, But Don't Be Simple

P. Griffith Lindell, Dean,
Hoff School of Business
Corban University

Today's Reading: Proverbs 9:1-6

Today's Key Verse: "Leave your simple ways and you will live; walk in the way of understanding" (Proverbs 9:6 NIV).

Today's Insights: I have been in business, counseled business people, and taught aspiring business leaders for more than forty years now. I dare say I've seen it all.

Yet one thing successful leaders have in common is *the desire to make wise decisions and to lead with integrity.* Where they differ from one another is how they go about their quest for this wisdom.

Consider today's reading—a description of Wisdom's feast. And check out these various translations of today's key verse: "Leave your impoverished confusion," "Forsake the foolish and simpleminded," "Leave your foolish ways behind," and "Forsake the foolish."

"Simple ways" is pregnant with meaning.

In studying today's reading, I was struck by the feast metaphor: God has done it all, even the getting of Wisdom. Of course I knew that, but the picture took on new color, new meaning. I don't have to slaughter the meat and cook it. I don't even have to set the table. I just have to come to dinner and feast!

"Sounds too simple," you may be thinking. "There's got to be stuff I need to *do* to get the wisdom I need to be a better leader."

The world's way is to *do, do, do*. Especially in business, we can't make progress if we're not taking initiative one way or another. So we look around us and get busy. Then again, to look straight down and read the Good Book, and to look straight up to speak with our good Father … how is that practical for running a business?

"The Bible is not a business book," some people assert.

Business school certainly gives the tools businessmen and women need to analyze, evaluate, and build organizational processes, but only a solidly Christian business school offers Wisdom and Understanding. Without

the latter, our ways are simple or foolish.
(Try telling *that* to a Harvard MBA!)

The truth is that the chief end of man is to
glorify God and enjoy Him forever, not to make
a profit. As one writer posited, ***"the goal of a
business is not profit. It is stewardship.
Profit results from good stewardship."***
I like that, for it says to me that even my
business is not "mine." Instead, it is His and
how I run it should reflect the Owner.

Even for a CEO of a public company, the
business is not "mine." Instead, it is "owned"
by shareholders, and the CEO is responsible for
being a steward of the assets of that company.
Those assets are not for him or her. Someone
else is always the owner! Who do you want to
own your company? God? Or someone else?

Whether at business school or the school of life,
any learning that leaves out God is foolish. It's
the simple (think simpleton) way.

What do we discover or learn if we "walk in the
way of understanding"? We can find a powerful
combination of learning from business school,
mentors and teachers, and God's Wisdom.

Yes, I know that many a business decision is
not right or wrong; rather, it's a matter of
which of two or more ethically right paths
should be followed.

Discerning those right paths takes Wisdom.
For we cannot see down a given path: following
God's lead is a walk of faith and not sight. And
I think we make "walking by faith" harder than
it needs to be; we tend to try to prepare the
meal, or at least to set the table.

Walking by faith is a walk of wisdom, a way of
understanding that begins with "knowing
God." This results from having a transparent
relationship with godly people, praying, and
feasting at the table of His Word.

The feast of wisdom is already prepared ... we
just have to show up and partake!

Are you hungry?

Dedicated to God

Greg Trull, Dean, School of Ministry
Corban University

Today's Reading: Romans 12:1-2

Today's Key Verse: "Therefore, I urge you, brothers, in view of God's mercy, to offer your bodies as living sacrifices, holy and pleasing to God—this is your spiritual act of worship" (Romans 12:1, NIVERSE1984).

Today's Insights: We were taking a break in the middle of a busy Israel tour day. Escaping the Jerusalem summer heat, I slipped into the Wohl Archaeological Museum. *As I paused to enjoy the cool air, I saw it. Barely the size of my hand. Broken after many uses. Buried for centuries. A powerful symbol of dedication.* I'd read about it but had never seen it for myself.

Beginning in 1968, Benjamin Mazar excavated south and southwest of the Temple Mount in Jerusalem. In the rubble fill near the southern wall, Mazar discovered a fragment of a stone cup from the first century. The cup had two doves etched on it just under four inscribed Hebrew letters: Q-R-B-N.

The Hebrew word *qorban* enjoys a rich history. The verb form refers to drawing near. Moses came near the camp of Israel and saw their celebration (Exodus 32:19). Esther came near the king to ask his favor (Esther 5:2). This concept of moving closer took on greater significance when the focus was the LORD. All eighty times the noun appears refer to sacrifices in worship.

The very first instructions for Israel's sacrificial worship introduced the idea of "corban."

> When any of you brings an offering [corban] to the LORD, bring as your offering [corban] an animal from either the herd or the flock (Leviticus 1:2).

After giving detailed orders for each of the offering types (Leviticus 1-7), Moses then summed up Israel's sacrificial worship with the word "corban."

> These are the regulations … for the Israelites to bring their offerings [corban] to the LORD (7:38-39).

With its crucial position in both the introduction and conclusion to sacrificial regulations, as well as its extensive use in reference to these offerings, ***"corban" stands***

as the central term for sacrifice in the Old Testament. It described the act of worshippers coming near to the LORD through a dedicated sacrifice.

In Jesus' time, worshippers set apart stone vessels to carry small sacrifices to the Temple. These cups, like the "corban" vessel, were inscribed as sacred. The presence of the two doves on the cup means it was likely used by parents bringing a sacrifice after the birth of a child. The Mishnah says new mothers would carry the cups with their sacrifices to the gates for the Court of Women.

Since women could not go beyond this court, a priest would meet them at the gate. He would take their sacrifices and offer them on their behalf. The sacrifice represented their faithful obedience to the Word and their worshipful devotion to the Lord. Mary and Joseph would have used a similar cup to dedicate Jesus at the Temple (Luke 2:22-24).

The ancient word qorban ("Corban" as we know it) also carries important truth for us today.

First, as Israelites came near the LORD, they did it by means of holy sacrifice. As Christians, we have been brought near to God by means of the holiest sacrifice, Jesus our Savior. "You who were once far away have been brought near through the blood of Christ" (Ephesians 2:13).

Second, those Old Testament offerings belonged to the LORD, dedicated to Him alone. Though Jesus has given the final and ultimate sacrifice for us, we still dedicate offerings to the Lord. Again, we see this in today's key verse: "I urge you, brothers, in view of God's mercy, to offer your bodies as living sacrifices, holy and pleasing to God" (Romans 12:1).

We continue to draw near to God, through Jesus Christ's final sacrifice, and offer ourselves as living sacrifices. We are gifts dedicated and brought before our awesome God.

4

Saltiness Is a Foundational Characteristic of the Christian

Jonathan Booth, Member, Executive Advisory Board, Hoff School of Business Corban University

Today's Reading: Matthew 5:1-12

Today's Key Verse: "You are the salt of the earth. But if the salt loses its saltiness, how can it be made salty again? It is no longer good for anything, except to be thrown out and trampled underfoot" (Matthew 5:13 NIV).

Today's Insights: We call it the "Sermon on the Mount," but maybe that doesn't do it justice. For us, a sermon is something to be repeated on a regular basis, but what was different about these words from the incarnate Son of God, Jesus Christ, was their uniqueness.

Jesus began by speaking of what it means to be truly blessed. The Beatitudes present eight blessings. Each is a proverb-like proclamation, without narrative, "cryptic, precise, and full of meaning. Each one includes a topic that forms a major biblical theme" (Allen Ross).

As you read these words, you will no doubt conclude that life as a Christian is clearly different from life *not* being a follower of Jesus Christ. But then ***Jesus turns the tables from a focus on our lives and us to what we are meant to be in the community we live in.*** He focuses on two things. First, the fact you and I are the salt of the earth. Second, the tragedy of salt losing its saltiness.

We are all aware of the difference salt makes to food when we either have or do not have salt. In modern times many have warned about too much salt but, in the right proportions, it is an essential part of making food the best it can be in terms of taste and enjoyment. Salt is a relatively small part of the food, but it is a powerful agent of change to every molecule of the food it permeates.

Jesus was often a direct communicator, and His communication style is no different here. He says, "You are the salt of the earth." ***What a great affirmation of the difference you can make to anything when you permeate everything around you.***

I met a man today who is running for political office—we need saltiness in politics. Another said he is the only Christian in the company he runs—we need saltiness in businesses.

Jesus Christ's commission tells us *we* are to reach the world. That means we are to be salty among our communities regardless of color or creed. When we make friends from other ethnic backgrounds rather than our own, we express the saltiness that Christ would have us purvey. In fact, there isn't anywhere on earth where we as followers of Christ cannot bring saltiness into whatever community we find ourselves.

The great affirmation that we are "the salt of the earth" is followed by this challenge: how awful it is to find a Christian who has lost that innate saltiness. Jesus Christ is urging His followers to consistency of faith and life.

Let's be mindful of who we will meet today, and let's be "the salt of the earth" in each and every encounter.

5

The Sin We Most Often Tolerate

Jim Hills, Professor of Humanities
Corban University

Today's Reading: James 4:1-10

Today's Key Verse: "Submit yourselves therefore to God. Resist the devil, and he will flee from you" (James 4:7 KJV).

Today's Insights: It is the sin, observed C. S. Lewis, that we find most repulsive in others but which we most often tolerate in ourselves. It made the list of seven deadly sins enumerated by the medieval church.

Indeed, pride—for this is what we are speaking of—appears to be the original sin in *heaven*, if we understand Ezekiel 28 correctly, and on *earth*, as indicated in Genesis 3. It is the root from which all other sins rise, the soil from which springs every poisonous weed in the human heart: lies, violence, adultery, theft, greed, fraud, malice, and on the grander scale of things, racism, genocide, and wars of conquest and subjugation.

What was the reason for the estimated 35 million deaths, military and civilian, in World War II, if not pride? In Europe and Asia, far too many people were willing to believe that they were members of a superior race and culture, and they followed the leaders who preached this lie straight to destruction.

It's an old lie—"you will be like gods yourselves." And ***the consequences are always the same: estrangement from God, estrangement from one another, and bitterness at every hand. And then anything is possible.***

For pride justifies every other sin.
King Ahab reasoned, *My neighbor's vineyard should be mine, for I am king.* David excused his adultery with the rationalization, *My friend's wife should be mine, for I am king.* Throughout the ages, emperors and common men have justified their sins against others by asserting their superiority.

The gifts of God are never enough for the proud. They believe they are entitled to more. The spouse, the job, the income, the church are never good enough. Even Eden, even heaven, not good enough. "From whence come wars and fightings among you?" James asked. Don't they come from our self-centered desires? And these desires, the appetites of the ungoverned ego, regard other people as means or as obstacles, to be used or to be overcome. **_People are loved for what advantage or service they can provide, which means, of course, they are loved not at all._**

The conduct of the Pharisees shows this point: they prayed, they tithed, they went often to the temple, but their righteous-looking behavior was less in the service of God than in the service of self.

They did all this, said Jesus, to be seen of men. And they got what they wanted. They got it even though they despised the very people for whose acclaim they lusted. They cared nothing for the penitent sinner; Pharisees need the publican to stay sinful so they can congratulate themselves on their own righteousness.

Nor were they pleased when a man took his first step in thirty-eight years (John 5). It seems that the healing had occurred outside the Pharisees' jurisdiction, and this, not the health of the healed man, was what mattered.

The biblical treatment prescribed for the sin of pride is not self-contempt or self-effacement. The quiet and shy may, in fact, be every bit as proud as the talkative and outgoing.

Pride is not a matter of personality; it is the central sin of the human spirit, and it must be treated as every other sin we

recognize in ourselves. We must learn to hate it as God hates it, to confess it, repent of it, to seek by the power of the Word and the Holy Spirit to root it out of our lives, and to grow the grace of humility in its place.

Left unchecked, pride separates and alienates people, as it alienated the first humans from one another, from their environment, and from God.

Few churches split over doctrinal issues. More commonly the rift grows out of what are politely called "personality clashes," collisions of egos and wills. Pride.

Imagine the absurdity, said Paul, of a proud eye saying to the hand, "I don't need you." When the eye and hand and head and feet fail to work together, we have a body that is diseased and crippled (1 Corinthians 12).

Let the people of God build, sing, teach, write, exhort, paint, cook, compose, run, grow flowers, lay brick, visit the sick, encourage the weak, all to the glory of the Redeemer.

For when we turn our attention to glorifying Him, we embrace true humility and repentance and come home to our Father's house.

6

We Are Servants

Janine Allen, Associate Provost of Global Engagement, Corban University

Today's Reading: 1 Corinthians 3:4-23

Today's Key Verse: "For no one can lay any foundation other than the one already laid, which is Jesus Christ" (1 Corinthians 3:11 NIV).

Today's Insights: The encouragement we receive from Paul in 1 Corinthians is focused on three elements challenging us to reflect on our true identity and motivation.

First, Paul questions who we are following and who we are serving. This is a good question! The names of great leaders in the marketplace, theologians in the church or seminary, teachers in the university and theorists are often referenced in daily conversations to give credibility for a way of thinking or behaving.

Even more, our behaviors are described based on specific human authors or a given leader. These ideas are communicated as principles of truth. Like the Corinthians Paul is exhorting, we hold these great thinkers and their track records of success as our reference points and metrics of success. And, before we know it, we have become consumers of human thoughts and human approval.

We strive to emulate another's way of life or his or her professional behavior. We even go so far as believing if we follow close enough, we will be successful and achieve great things. Whose standard are we following?

Paul raises the questions, "For when one says, 'I follow Paul,' and another, 'I follow Apollos,' are you not mere human beings? What, after all, is Apollos? And what is Paul? Only servants, through whom you came to believe— as the Lord has assigned to each his task" (1 Corinthians 3:4-5).

We must keep in perspective that great thinkers are placed by God and used by God for specific purposes. It is not their wisdom or discovered truth, after all, but revelation from the Truth Himself.

Jesus says, "I am the way, the truth and life" (John 14:6). We must keep in perspective that we are followers, not of other people, but of Jesus Christ, who freely uses His created beings for God's kingdom purposes. Again, we are *His* servants, not servants of man.

What then are our metrics of success?
We need to evaluate ourselves and make

certain our measure is based on Jesus Christ
and our lives are based on the Word of God.
Instead of being a fan of a human leader—
becoming a consumer and building our thought
life and behaviors based on another—we are
called to be servants of Jesus Christ.

It is dangerous to try to follow and emulate
anyone else, relinquishing life's authority to
someone who is fallen. Instead, our life metric
and behaviors must be based on God's Word.

"So then, no more boasting about human
leaders! All things are yours, whether Paul or
Apollos or Cephas or the world or life or death
or the present or the future—all are yours, and
you are of Christ, and Christ is of God"
(1 Corinthians 3:21-23). Our foundation must
be Jesus Christ—the simplicity and purity of
God's Son.

A second encouragement from Paul is
based on our individual roles in the gospel
community. We are co-laborers and must build
the church together. Our unity is essential for
growth. Some plant the seeds, others water,
weed, or nourish. The foundation of the church
is not based on human behaviors; one calling is
not greater than another.

We must humble ourselves to be used by Jesus
to accomplish His good and perfect will. As
Jesus reminds His disciples when on earth,

"The words that I say to you, I do not speak on my own authority, but the Father who dwells in me does his works" (John 14:10).

On earth, God's Son followed and responded to the Father. Should we not do the same? The opposite is a narcissistic evangelistic mission based on our own purposes and ideas. If we are not careful, we will elevate ourselves based on our personal goals and admiration instead of Jesus Christ.

The third point Paul makes is: we are temples. "Don't you know that you yourselves are God's temple and that God's Spirit dwells in your midst?" (1 Corinthians 3:16). Our daily surrender to the Father—recognizing that our identity is in Jesus Christ—is our true worship.

How do we embody the dwelling place of Jesus? As Jesus did, we must be humble and empty ourselves and find our identity in the Father. We are followers and servants of the highest God, Creator of all that is.

7

Do You Recall the Day?

*Bill Pugh, Vice President for Advancement
Corban University*

Today's Reading: Ephesians 2:4-10

Today's Key Verse: "But because of his great love for us, God, who is rich in mercy, made us alive with Christ" (Ephesians 2:4-5a NIV).

Today's Insights: Do you remember the day God came looking for you? Can you recall that life-changing day when you first placed your faith in Jesus Christ? *Is there a day when God first intervened in your life, bringing you a whole new level of contentment, peace, and joy?*

A spring afternoon in the early 1980s will forever be a spiritual marker in my life. I was a junior at the University of Maryland, playing football for the Terrapins. (Go Terps!) On this particular day, I had retreated to my dorm room after a physically draining spring practice session.

As I relaxed in my room—located on the eighth floor of my dormitory—enjoying adult beverages and listening to Lynyrd Skynyrd, there was a knock on my door. I opened the door to find a Campus Crusade for Christ (Cru) staff member, Steve Holt, requesting to come in and tell me how I could have a personal relationship with Jesus Christ.

I thought to myself, *What would be the harm in letting this former collegiate gymnast come in and talk with me about Jesus?* He weighed only 125 pounds soaking wet, and if the conversation went south, I could always hang my personal proselytizer out the window by his feet and he'd surely recant and (like others before him) not return. After all, I *was* living on the eighth floor.

As Mr. Holt began talking, however, I found myself intently listening. He talked about the fact that God had created me and that He made me to know Him and live according to His plan and purpose for my life. The problem was most people—certainly including me—choose to live independently from God and in opposition to His plan and purpose for their lives.

I had no problem identifying with the concept of independence from God (what Mr. Holt referred to as "sin," missing God's intended mark for our lives). Every time I chose to veer from God's purposeful course, to walk away, declaring my independence from him, it was like taking a dull knife and dragging it across my heart, further desensitizing me from being able to discern, listen to and respond to God's still small voice.

So it was on this divinely appointed day, in the spring of 1981, that God prepared my heart to respond to Him. I answered with a resounding "yes" to God's invitation to come home and personally accept what Jesus did on my behalf. For the first time in my life, I yielded to God's offer of forgiveness through Jesus Christ. I moved from trusting *me* to trusting Christ, who had paid the price for my sins by dying on the cross.

I repeated a short prayer that day, and it came straight from my heart. I said something similar to this: ***"Heavenly Father, thank You for opening my eyes this day to the reality of who You are. Thank You for sending Your Son to die on the cross to pay the penalty for my sin. I ask You to forgive me for my sins—past, present, and future. Now take control of my life. Make me who You want me to be."***

I have recalled that moment—the moment where Jesus Christ first became real in my life—countless times. It really is amazing how God reaches down and restores a broken relationship with us.

Grace is God granting us what we could never

earn or deserve (Ephesians 2:8-9), and I see today how grace gave me both the chance to personally know Him, and the chance today to pursue getting to know Him better.

The apostle Paul reminds us that of all our lofty goals, the pre-eminent one must be to "know Him [Jesus Christ] and the power of His resurrection and the fellowship of sharing in His sufferings, being conformed to His death" (Philippians 3:10 NASB).

I am also acutely aware of the fact that God came looking for me, because I wasn't looking for Him. As Jesus said, "You did not choose me, but I chose you" (John 15:16 NIV).

The Lord's grace restores me and gives me daily sustaining power—physically, emotionally, and spiritually. It is by His grace that I come to the cross and by His grace that I move forward in the journey He daily sets before me (Ephesians 2:10).

All these years later, every day still is by Him, for Him, and always focused on being about Him!

8

Right Now and Into Eternity

Sheldon C. Nord, President
Corban University

Today's Reading: Mark 8:3-9a

Today's Key Verse: "And other seeds fell into good soil and produced grain, growing up and increasing and yielding thirtyfold and sixtyfold and a hundredfold" (Mark 4:8 ESV).

Today's Insights: Corban University is unapologetically Christian. We care as much about the kind of person each student is becoming as what kind of job he or she will eventually get, and as much about how he will do his job as about which job he does.

In his inimitable style, C. S. Lewis wrote: "Now there are a good many things which would not be worth bothering about if I were going to live only seventy years, but which I had better bother about very seriously if I am going to live forever."

Eternal consequences shape how we provide education, how we live our

**lives, and how we do business around
the globe.**

In Scripture, we find in Jesus a man who lived
in light of eternity, but not at the expense of the
present. He did not dismiss physical human
needs because they were somehow irrelevant in
the grand scheme of living forever.

No, Jesus Himself had physical needs, and He
gladly met those of the people around Him, as
we see in today's reading. He satisfied hunger
pangs, and not just spiritually because He is
the Bread of Life from heaven, but physical
pangs that actually gnaw at our guts.

Jesus does not belittle us for being human.
**He challenges us to be fully present as
we too pursue a life that will last into
eternity.**

This approach in life creates a tension, but it is
one into which we are privileged to live.

Without it, we might err on the side of a "holier
than thou" approach to life, or on the other end
of the spectrum, a superficiality that shackles
us to this world.

Richard J. Foster has noted:

> Superficiality is the curse of our age.
> The doctrine of instant satisfaction is

a primary spiritual problem. The desperate need today is not for a greater number of intelligent people, or gifted people, but for deep people.

Any journey at sea, of any length, will bring wind, rain, rough waters, and other challenges. Today we need more university graduates who can navigate the storms of life because they have a strong and reliable rudder—a deep and abiding relationship with Jesus Christ and the truth of His Word. We all face challenges, in our personal health and wellness, at work, at home, and in our church involvements.

I have a burden that we prepare the next generation to live their lives with boldness and confidence, not because of what they can do but because of Who they serve. We want to prepare them for the storms of life.

This deep living is what motivates us at Corban. We are a university focused on preparing deep people for a lifetime of service to their communities to the glory of God. We are about attracting, challenging, training, and educating the leaders of tomorrow.

I am convinced that lasting change begins and ends with Jesus Christ. He is the One who changes hearts, minds, lives, communities and nations. He is the One through whom all of life's questions can be filtered, wrestled with, and resolved.

Throughout American history, a number of colleges and universities have been concerned about more than what their students know; they have also cared to influence the kind of people they become.

At Corban, we are committed to pouring into every aspect of our students' lives—mind, heart, body, and soul. You will witness this at music and theatre performances, in the classroom, on the athletic field, and in the dining hall. The soil for growing a healthy crop expands across every inch of our beautiful 142-acre campus.

As Christians, Jesus Christ is continually pressing into us, longing to draw us closer to His heart.

So, I must ask:

- Are you living fully in the present, with your heart set on eternity?

- Are you pressing into the call to be a deep, mission-driven person who strives for nothing short of bringing God glory in every decision, interaction, and pursuit?

Let's never forget: We serve an awesome God who loves us wholly and completely, and who desires nothing short of our entire being— mind, heart, body, and soul.

That's why Corban's mission is ***"To educate Christians who will make a difference in the world for Jesus Christ"*** (based on Matthew 28:19-20) because what the world needs, quite simply, is more of Him.

9

How We Are Made New

*Matt Lucas, Provost/
Executive Vice President
Corban University*

Today's Reading: 2 Corinthians 5:16-21

Today's Key Verse: "Therefore, if anyone is in Christ, he is a new creation. The old has passed away; behold the new has come" (2 Corinthians 5:17 NIV).

Today's Insights: If any verse succinctly captures the power of the gospel to bring about personal transformation, it is this verse. It simultaneously looks at the beginning and end of history as we know it.

First, it looks at the opening chapters of Genesis and evokes the grandeur of God's creative act where He spoke into nothing and created a universe.

At the same time this verse anticipates the last chapters of Revelation where John describes the new heavens and new earth.

As one redeemed by Jesus Christ, I marvel that the same power to create the universe, and

34

bring down the new Jerusalem, brings about the transformation of me.

And yet, I find the old me ever present: my body veers from godly intentions, my mind wanders in paths that stray from the truth, and my heart pursues idols that lead me toward destruction.

My futile attempts at personal transformation always lead to two dead-ends: an impotent attempt at good works and the creation of a new system of rules (always a form of legalism). The apostle Paul clearly reminds you and me that neither results in reformation.

> If with [Jesus] Christ you died to the elemental spirits of the world, why, as if you were still alive in the world, do you submit to regulations—"Do not handle, Do not taste, Do not touch" (referring to things that all perish as they are used)—according to human precepts and teachings? These have indeed an appearance of wisdom in promoting self-made religion and asceticism and severity to the body, but they are of no value in stopping the indulgence of the flesh (Colossians 2:20-23).

So, what do I do if I can't turn to self-imposed rules? The answer simply is that I do nothing.

Thankfully, I have a Savior who is not just interested in making me right with God, but also in making me holy in his sight.

To put it theologically, the cause of my justification is the source of my sanctification.

To put it practically, before I came to Jesus Christ, I was helpless to make myself right before God; therefore, there was nothing I could do to win His affection. After coming to Jesus Christ, I am still helpless to transform myself into the likeness of my Savior.

I find that after years of living the Christian life, I'm still perplexed at the mystery of the gospel's transformation of me. What must happen to my head, heart and hands? I believe Ephesians 3:16-19 provides one of the clearest explanations of how that transformation occurs.

> that according to the riches of his glory
>
> he strengthens me with power through his [Holy] Spirit in my inner being
>
> so that [Jesus] Christ may dwell in my heart through faith

that I may have strength to
comprehend what is the breadth and

length and height and depth of
Christ's love, which surpasses all
knowledge

so that I may be filled with all the
fullness of God [the Father].

In this Scripture passage, we see each person of
the Trinity intimately involved in our
transformation.

In the end, we do nothing.

Instead, I simply invite the Lord God, creator
of heaven and earth, to use His almighty power
to renew my mind in its thinking, to reshape
my heart in its affections, and to redirect my
hands in their activities.

Are you submitting to God so that He can do
the same for you?

10

The Unexpected

Marty Trammell, Chair of Humanities
Corban University

Today's Reading: Luke 7:1-19.

Today's Key Verse: "Summoning two of his disciples, John sent them to the Lord, saying, 'Are you the Expected One, or do we look for someone else?'" (Luke 7:19 NASB).

Today's Insights: We don't know much about the boy Jesus. Did He take bread to His dad in the carpenter's shop? Did He play in the streets with friends?

Did He make things with His hands like His father? Did He whittle away some of His hours or help His mom with the children? Did she teach Him how to wash His hands or carry water? Did she show Him how to bind a wound? Did His dad teach Him how to finish a table or how to forgive the debts of customers who couldn't afford to pay?

Did He learn to debate and defend Himself? Or was He silent when accused? At the yearly sacrifice, did He ever watch his father lead a lamb to the slaughter? We don't know.

What we do know is that as a boy, Jesus wanted to spend time in His Father's house. This small town kid walked through the big city streets of Jerusalem, trading its amazements for conversations with teachers.

And, we know He wasn't always where people expected Him to be. His mom and dad found Him in the temple one afternoon when they expected Him to be with family and friends. He seemed to live His life that way—constantly found in places the people around Him thought inappropriate.

Despite the advice of His friends and family, He spent time with the homeless and tax collectors, priests and prostitutes—often somewhere unexpected. Maybe, John the Baptist's question was really a statement: "Are you the Expected One?"

The boy, Jesus, lived an unexpected life—a characteristic He never outgrew in the thirty-three years earth knew Him. As the gospels show us, even those closest to Him didn't expect crucifixion. Do you see the point here?

In following Jesus, God often calls us to do the unexpected.

When atheists at work expect us to avoid those from other religious backgrounds and lifestyles, do we do the unexpected?

When the religious leaders of our day expect us to patronize their platforms and parties, do we do the unexpected?

When social outcasts and the disenfranchised need a friend, do we choose, instead, to hang out with those who might benefit us in some way? That's expected.

Like our Lord, are we what people expect or what they need?

Ron Hall said, "Most people want to be circled by safety, not by the unexpected. The unexpected can take you out. But the unexpected can also take you over and change your life. Put a heart in your body where a stone used to be."

It's strange that Jesus never answers John's question with a "yes." Instead He tells John's disciples to return to him and tell him about all that Jesus was doing. Jesus didn't deliver John from prison or free God's chosen from tyranny like John might have hoped. Instead, He restored sight to the blind, healed the lame and lepers, caused the deaf to hear and raised the dead. And He preached the gospel to the poor.

So much unexpected from the Expected One.

11

Maybe We Are All on a Need-to-Know Basis

Mark A. Jacobson, Associate Professor of Theology, Corban University

Today's Reading: John 14:1-6

Today's Key Verse: "I am the way, the truth and the life. No one comes to the Father except through me" (John 14:6 NIV).

Today's Insights: I have always felt sorry for the apostle Thomas, who becomes the foil for one of the most well-known and profound sayings of Jesus recorded by John (today's key verse). Thomas, after all, was asking Jesus to clarify something that was quite important but that needed to be clarified. After all, Jesus had just announced that He was about to leave them, but one day He would return and receive them to Himself.

Jesus' announcement is anything but clear. He told His disciples, hours before the climactic events that would result in His death, that they should not be troubled, that He was leaving them to prepare a place for them in His Father's house, that He would return to them and receive them (as His guests), and that where He was they would be also.

If this wasn't vague enough, Jesus concludes with the statement, recorded in verse 4: "And you know the way where I am going." At least the best manuscript evidence indicates that this is what Jesus said.

If you've grown up with the KJV, as I have, you're more familiar with this version of verse 4: "And wither I go ye know, and the way ye know." With the addition of "and" and another "you know," Jesus' statement is more along the line of what we might expect Him to have said.

When I do a Google search for a driving destination, I have both the destination and the way to get there marked out on the map. But the manuscript evidence seems to favor the shorter statement, "And you know the way where I am going." If I had my choice, I would choose to have a clear idea of both where I am going and also the way that gets me there.

Thomas had the same desire: "Lord, we do not know where you are going; how can we know the way?" In Thomas's thinking, you can't answer one question without answering the other. But while Jesus is vague on the former, He is not on the latter.

Who among us, as followers of Jesus, doesn't

want to know where we are headed? We all would like some insights into where God is leading us in our careers, ministries, relationships, etc.

Yet I have learned, over the course of my 40+ years of serving the Lord, that I'm not on a need-to-know basis for what lies ahead. What lies ahead, whether in the next few years or for our life to come, is not what Jesus said I know. What I do know is "the Way."

Eventually I will "come to the Father," whatever that means; that part is a little hazy, just as what lies ahead in the immediate future. But for me, and for all my colleagues and students at Corban seeking to know God's will for them in the future, it is enough to know the Way, wherever that Way will take us.

12

How Much Grace Did It Take to Save You?

Kevin Brubaker, Vice President for Business, Corban University

Today's Reading: 1 Timothy 1:12-17

Today's Key Verse: "The saying is trustworthy and deserving of full acceptance, that Christ Jesus came into the world to save sinners, of whom I am the foremost" (1 Timothy 1:15 ESV).

Today's Insights: I lived a horrible, sinful, rebellious life until that moment when Jesus Christ called me to be His own. Then I turned six.

Maybe that is your testimony as well. I lack the story of an ugly life apart from Christ. If you want me to share "my story" you probably won't be wowed by it. Because of that, it is easy for me to look at the testimony of Paul and marvel. How amazing that God could save someone so lost and so evil!

Ah, but you see what I've done. I've made myself someone worth saving, or at least a little

44

easier to save. Because I wasn't all that bad when Jesus Christ saved me, He must have suffered just a little less when He paid for my sin than He did for Paul's sin.

When I share the gospel with someone who is entrenched in the ugliness of sin, they may ask, "How can God save someone like me?" I can say, "Well, if God saved Paul, He can save you." Certainly, I wouldn't use myself as an example, for I was a little easier to save!

But is that true? And is the point of the passage that God saved an awful sinner like Paul?

The heart of Paul's message about himself is in verse 15. Note the use of the present tense: "Christ Jesus came into the world to save sinners of whom I *am* the foremost." Many commentators are quick to point out that Paul certainly couldn't have been saying he *is* a terrible sinner after salvation. He was pointing to his pre-salvation life with that comment. But Paul knew how to write and he could have easily used the past tense as he did in verses 12-14. Why didn't he?

I believe Paul knew two things about himself that are true of any of us. First, he knew that his post-salvation life was a result of God's work and not his own efforts. Apart from the work of the Spirit in his life he would still be that same sinner he was before salvation.

Second, he knew that he still sins constantly.

What is the greatest commandment? "Love the Lord your God with all your heart, all your soul and all your mind." Ever fall short of that commandment? How often? The more mature in Christ we become, the more we are made aware of the greatness of God's righteousness and the depth of our own sin.

All of us, like Paul, were saved by God's grace and mercy. All of us, like Paul, can say that God is at work in our lives but, in and of ourselves, we fall woefully short of God's standard. And all of us, like Paul can say that God displays in us His perfect patience as an example to those who would believe.

My challenge to you today: personalize this passage. Appreciate the grace of God that saved you from your sin. Allow yourself, like Paul, to be a billboard that advertises the grace of God that saves sinners like Paul, you and me.

13

Humility

Jim Hills, Professor of Humanities
Corban University

Today's Reading: Philippians 2:5-11.

Today's Key Verse: "Let this mind be in you, which was also in Christ Jesus" (Philippians 2:5 KJV).

Today's Insights: Of the classic Christian virtues humility may be the least understood. It is sometimes mistakenly equated with timidity, shyness, or self-deprecation.

But it is none of these. Moses was not being humble in the biblical sense when he resisted God's commission. It's clear that God did not regard Moses' reluctance as stemming from genuine humility. Indeed, "the anger of the Lord was kindled against Moses" (Exodus 4:14).

It was time for the people of Israel to be delivered from Egypt, cross the wilderness and make new homes in Canaan. For this great enterprise they needed a great leader. If not Moses, then who? False humility was not called for; confident obedience was.

Humility is not the opposite of godly confidence; it is the opposite of self-aggrandizement. Genuinely humble Christians understand that they have been given talents, gifts and training to be used in the service of others. Paul never introduced himself as Paul the scholar or Paul the writer, but as "a servant of Jesus Christ, called to be an apostle."

"Let nothing be done through strife or vain glory," he wrote the Christians in Philippi, "but in lowliness of mind let each esteem others better than themselves."

Learning at its best is an act of self-forgetfulness. The lab experiment, the poem and the history lesson are interesting and valuable in their own right, not merely for how they may relate to the student.

God has granted us in creation all the dignity we need. Godly humility recognizes, with the psalmist, that human beings are "crowned with glory and honor," rulers "over the works of [God's] hands ... flocks and herds, and the beasts of the field, the birds of the air, and the fish of the sea" (Psalm 8).

There is no need, then, for us to be vigilant in defending the borders of our psyches. The biblically humble person is a free person, free from the cynical calculus of ego enhancement, free from the shabby gray walls of defensiveness, free to enjoy and celebrate the gifts and accomplishments of others created in God's image, and free to serve.

Humility, like love, does not keep score, but finds joy in service itself. Jesus said of the arrogant and self-righteous Pharisees, "all their works they do for to be seen of men ... [T]hey love ... greetings in the markets, and to be called of men, Rabbi, Rabbi. But be not ye called Rabbi: for one is your master, even Christ; and all ye are brethren ... and whosoever shall exalt himself shall be abased; and he that shall humble himself shall be exalted" (Matthew 23).

This humility is not, to be sure, the way to win a presidential election; it is the way to live a loving and joyful life honoring to the Lord and to one another. For the biblically humble, service is an ordinary disposition. They do what should be done without thinking much about it and without keeping track.

But God keeps track. One day, said Jesus, the king will say to the quietly righteous, "Come, ye blessed of my Father, inherit the kingdom prepared for you ... for I was an hungered, and ye gave me meat: I was thirsty and ye gave me drink: I was a stranger, and ye took me in: naked, and ye clothed me: I was sick, and ye visited me: I was in prison, and ye came to me."

The response of the righteous is revealing: "We did? When?" Jesus' answer is well-known: "Inasmuch as ye have done it unto the least of these my brethren, ye have done it unto me" (Matthew 25).

Genuine humility is at heart the recognition that nothing is our own to do with as we merely please—not our money, nor our talents, nor our time, nor our selves. All are gifts from God, expressions of His creativity and generosity.

And finally it all flows back to Him. In the end there is no egotism, no hanging back, no thought of self at all, only the casting of crowns before Him and the eternal confession: "Thou art worthy, O Lord, to receive glory and honour and power. For thou hast created all things, and for thy pleasure they are and were created." Amen.

14

Enough Is Enough

*Nathan Geer, Dean of Students
Corban University*

Today's Reading: Exodus 16:13-25.

Today's Key Verse: "When they measured it with an omer, he who had gathered much had no excess, and he who had gathered little had no lack; every man gathered as much as he should eat" (Exodus 16:18 NASB).

Today's Insights: Enough. It is a difficult word to define. It changes and fluctuates depending on a variety of factors: family size, environment, capacity of the container, length of the drought. There are many reasons why enough may differ between people. Thankfully we have a loving Father who understands our need.

As the children of Israel sought sustenance in the Wilderness, the LORD provided specifically as each had need. Families with many children never ran short. Single individuals had no excess. The measure was right for each. And as families and individuals followed the instruction there was health and protection.

Only when greed arose and people attempted to provide for themselves and their future did worms and corruption creep in and destroy.

Excess is not in the Divine vocabulary.

In Matthew 6:11, Jesus urges His disciples to pray, "Give us this day, our daily bread," hearkening back to the enough of Exodus and daily manna. We were not created to provide for ourselves, but to rely on "everything that proceeds out of the mouth of the LORD" (Deuteronomy 8:3). He is our sustenance, our provider, our protection, our eternity and He always provides enough.

The truth of this passage lands heavily in an age and culture of excess. From television screen size to choice of channels. From digital storage space to the size of standard dinner plates. Our appetites grow as quickly as our society can produce. The images and messages surrounding us only urge us to consume and devour more and more. Drought pushes us to dig deeper and deeper within the earth to find water. At what point do we draw the line and cry, "Enough!"

The difficulty lies in that last word. Enough is in the hands of the Father. It is not ours to determine for one another. As each person or family puts faith and trust in God, He will provide enough for their need. He desires that we continually rely on Him for our need and not on our own cleverness, understanding or ability to provide.

True, we need to do our part and gather the provisions (plant, water, cultivate, etc.), but the harvest comes from His hand. When we feel we have too little, faith gives thanks for the enough He has provided.

Retirement has always been an enigma to me. Saving and saving for the future so there will come a time in life when I no longer have need of anyone or anything and can wholly depend on my own efforts to relax and do my own bidding. I fear this flies in the face of the provision the Father desires for us.

He wants us to remain in relationship with Him until our final breath and He also wants us connected to one another until this moment. Provision for the future is already secured in Christ. As we trust in Him our needs are met day by day on into eternity.

So the next time you are encouraged to super-size your meal or pay a little extra for more gigabytes of capacity, consider the manna provided by your heavenly Father and ask yourself how much is enough.

Do not let a culture of excess distract you from the provision of the Lord. Give Him first place

and seek daily to have the enough He provides.
For those who follow this path and gather
much will have no excess, and those who
gather little will have no lack.

They will simply have enough.

15

Thankful for Community

Sheldon C. Nord, President
Corban University

Today's Reading: Hebrews 10:19-25.

Today's Key Verse: "As iron sharpens iron, so one person sharpens another" (Proverbs 27:17 NIV).

Today's Insights: I have learned a lot the past three years ... a lot about matters of importance facing Corban University, a lot about myself, a lot about the Lord, and a lot about the people around me. Through it all, the value of *community* has nudged its way to the top of the list of things for which I am grateful.

"No man is an island" and this truth is evident everywhere on our campus, from Schimmel to the dining hall, from the C. E. Jeffers Sports Center to the amphitheatre, from the residence halls to the classrooms, from the library to the Emitte Center, and from the Psalm Performing Arts Center to the athletic fields.

We are better when we are in community. When we allow ourselves to be molded and refined by others, we avoid the rough edges that come from isolation and an unhealthy sense of independence. When we let people into our lives—and not in a superficial way, but at the level where heart change truly happens—that's when we experience what the Bible refers to as "iron sharpening iron." We grow. We sharpen. We become the men and women God intends us to be.

When we lived in Karawaci, Indonesia, approximately 20 kilometers west of Jakarta, it was challenging at times to deal with a different language, different cultural traditions, daily prayers being offered at the local mosque, and the humidity ... mostly the heat and humidity. We were surrounded by a community of local colleagues, as well as a pretty sizable group of "expats" from Canada, Australia and the U.S.A.

These relationships, and the amazing fellowship that came with them, sustained us and were a tremendous source of energy and encouragement to us. It didn't take away the challenges and difficulty, but did insert joy in spite of the circumstances. This sense of community made all the difference.

Jesus Christ Himself was a man of community. Within the Trinity, the Son is naturally one with the Father and Holy Spirit. The communion they experience is constant and intimate. And during His time on earth, Jesus made a point to surround Himself with His select group of 12, the disciples who literally walked alongside Him through His years of ministering to others and sharing the gospel. We learn from Him the value of community, of doing life with others and caring for one another as brothers and sisters.

When our students look at their yearbooks each spring, they quickly scan the faces of those who have become part of their community at Corban. They also quickly realize they are not the same people they were in the fall. God has been shaping and growing them as His children. He has used coaches, professors, staff, peers and members of the Salem community to help shape them more into the image of His Son, Jesus Christ.

As Corban means "a gift dedicated to God," may we count each person in our life a great gift given to us by God.

16

Success vs. Significance

Greg Eide, Director of Athletics
Corban University

Today's Reading: Hebrews 13:15-21

Today's Key Verse: "Do not neglect to do good and to share what you have, for such sacrifices are pleasing to God" (Hebrews 13:16 ESV).

Today's Insights: Have you ever taken a moment to consider what others will say about you at your memorial service? If an epitaph were written on your tombstone, what would it say?

Like most other people who grow up in our American culture, it seems as if we are encouraged to be successful in everything that we do from the minute we breathe our first breath.

When I look back over my own life, I certainly followed this pursuit of success. I desired to be a successful student, a successful athlete, a successful son, a successful businessman, a successful husband, a successful father, and so on.

As a Christian, it was very easy for me to follow this pursuit as I had been raised to give the Lord my best shot in everything that I do and to pursue excellence at all times. In Colossians 3, we are instructed, whenever we work, to do that work as if we are working for the Lord.

My family, especially my father, would accept nothing less. He had grown up during the Depression, a son to parents from Norway and Sweden who hopped on separate boats headed to Ellis Island to chase the American dream.

Looking back, I was blessed to achieve success in many of these pursuits. However, as I started reaching my 50s, I felt something was missing. A friend suggested I read Bob Buford's book, "Halftime." Buford challenges us in the second half of our lives to begin shifting our focus from success to significance.

This hit a chord with me. Was I going to continue to focus my efforts on continued success, or try and shift my focus on utilizing that success to impact other's lives in a significant way?

It would require me to take the next step. Although I believed that I had had a significant impact on lives around me, it was more a by-product of being successful, than due to an intentional effort.

If I was willing to make myself available to be used by the Lord, what could be accomplished to make this world a better place? After much prayer, I decided I was going to go all in on this pursuit of significance.

The past decade, I can honestly say, has been the most fulfilling period of my life. I have not given up my pursuit of excellence, or my pursuit of success, which is woven in my DNA and I believe is the way God created me. It has been achieved as a result of pursuing a life of significance.

Now when I am provided an investment opportunity, or a way to use my time, I ask myself how I can use this for others rather than purely for personal gain.

One of my favorite quotes is, "The life worth living is a life lived for others."

Back to the epitaph ... I invite you to write ten words others would currently etch to describe your life. Then ponder those words for a few minutes.

Is it time for a shift in focus? Is your life having a significant impact on others?

Consider asking the Lord to help you have an even greater outward view on life. Hebrews 13:16 says, "Do not neglect to do good and to share what you have, for such sacrifices are pleasing to God."

All God's best as you pursue a life well-lived for the Lord and one that significantly impacts others along the way!

17

Contemplating Infinity

*Pam Teschner, Associate Provost of
Academics, Corban University*

Today's Reading: Psalm 19:1-6, 107:1-3, 43

Today's Key Verse: "Consider the great love
of the LORD" (Psalm 107:43b NASB).

Today's Insights: Wrapping my mind
around the love of God is like trying to
contemplate infinity. It's like peering deep into
the star-studded night sky and imagining
endlessness.

To consider the great love of God is to ponder
the eternal uncreated Existence before the
beginning ... before earth ... before stars and
space dust ... before angels ... before
everything.

A brief flicker of eternity illuminates the
darkness of my mind for an instant, and my
soul gasps at the fleeting light.

My mind reaches to describe it, but it vanishes
beyond words and paradigms. The vastness of
eternity somehow resides within my being and
is etched upon my soul.

The immense ocean of His love floods and overflows my small heart. It swells with the unimaginable fullness of His love until, enraptured and overwhelmed, it nearly bursts.

This is but a modicum of His love, and if I should glimpse its complete fullness, I would perish in the crush of its glory.

Every fiber of the Eternal God stretches out after me. Before everything, He chose me and called me to Himself.

He intends me to experience the indescribable joy of His Presence in the innermost core of my soul—His heart beating within mine, and mine within His. That kind of love is far too weighty for my puny mind to grasp.

He relentlessly pursues this mortal bundle of bones with all its failings, and is satisfied with nothing less than every cell of it. He knocks at the door of my heart gently but persistently.

Hearing His voice, I fuss about attempting to tidy up the disarray of my heart to make it fit for the King's entrance.

Embarrassed and ashamed, I try desperately to clean out the dust and dirt of life. Hard as I might, I can't shake it off my feet but continue tracking it through the rooms of my heart.

In complete poverty of spirit and trembling faith, I crack open the door of my disheveled life. In utter amazement, I am swept up and enveloped by God Himself. Glory dawns over my soul.

In that moment I know I am His and He is mine ... no matter what.

18

I Doubt It

Kent Kersey, Professor of Theology
Corban University

Today's Reading: John 20:24–31

Today's Key Verse: "Jesus said to him,
'Because you have seen Me, have you
believed? Blessed are they who did not see,
and yet believed'" (John 20:29 NASB).

Today's Insights: Doubting Thomas is the
one disciple who made some bold demands. He
refused to believe his colleagues' outrageous
claims about seeing Jesus alive.

In hindsight we know Thomas should have
believed them because they were right, yet we
shouldn't judge Thomas too harshly.

If you put yourself in his shoes, would you have
fared any better? I doubt I would.

Consider Thomas' state of mind. He witnessed
the violent torture of his teacher. His mentor
was dead. He lost his best friend.

Thomas was not cold-hearted. He was brokenhearted.

The last stanza of a famous poem by W. H. Auden might give some insight about how Thomas might have been feeling.

> The stars are not wanted now: put out
>   every one;
> Pack up the moon and dismantle the
>   sun;
> Pour away the ocean and sweep up the
>   wood.
> For nothing now can ever come to any
>   good.[1]

Thomas was not a skeptical academic debating the existence of God. He was a tenderhearted companion mourning the loss of his dear friend. This story, fortunately, has a happy ending. Jesus shows up and Thomas becomes a true believer.

Here are a few observations about how Thomas turned from a doubter to a believer. These ideas can also help our faith today.

First of all, Thomas was honest. His candid confession might be shocking, but it was also the key to his powerful encounter with Jesus. If he had never admitted his inability to believe, he wouldn't have had the opportunity to become a true believer.

---

[1] https://web.cs.dal.ca/~johnston/poetry/stopclocks.html

We need to encourage the development of communities which foster fierce honesty. We need to be the type of people who can safely receive honest confessions of doubt. After all, doubt is not sin. Doubt is, in fact, the flip side of faith.

Blaise Pascal once said: "Seeing too much to deny and too little to be sure, I am in a state to be pitied." This sentiment can be echoed by many sincere Christians who have had powerful experiences which build their faith whilst also living in a world that often makes it hard to believe.

Secondly, Thomas put himself in a position to be blessed. Even though Thomas was in a state of doubt, he refused to isolate himself. Verse 26 tells us that "Thomas was with them."

Even though Thomas thought that Jesus' resurrection was too good to be true, he decided to hang out where Jesus was most likely to show up if He really were alive.

Thomas was with the disciples. In moments of doubt and despair it's best to be with God's people. Hopefully you and I are cultivating communities where doubters can hang out with believers.

Thirdly, Thomas learned the true meaning of faith. Jesus tells us that the ones who believe without seeing are blessed. The word "blessed" is incredibly powerful. It doesn't simply mean happy. The best translation of the Greek word is "fully satisfied."

Jesus tells us, then, that we can only be fully satisfied when we believe without seeing. In fact, we can only be satisfied in our faith when we accept that the key to a strong belief is focusing on the object of our faith rather than the strength of our faith.

Many of us wish that we had stronger faith. However, Jesus says that the smallest amount of faith can do the most miraculous things. You can have a lot of faith in thin ice and fall through; you can have very little faith in thick ice and literally walk on water.

The key to building our faith, then, is to honestly voice our doubts amongst God's people who look to Jesus as the only worthy object of our faith.

19

What Do Penguins Have to Do with Psalm 8?

Sam Baker, Associate Professor of Ministries, Corban University

Today's Reading: Psalm 8

Today's Key Verse: "When I consider Your heavens, the work of Your fingers, The moon and the stars, which You have ordained; What is man that You take thought of him, And the son of man that You care for him? Yet You have made him a little lower than God, And You crown him with glory and majesty!" (Psalm 8:3-5 NASB).

Today's Insights: Have you seen *The March of the Penguins*? When you watch the movie, you instantly become fascinated by the story and the amazing details regarding Emperor Penguins.

Some of those interesting details, as compiled by Emanuel Levy:

- The Emperor Penguin uses a particular spot as their breeding ground because it is on pack ice that is solid year round, so there is no danger of the ice becoming too soft to support the colony.

- It is also in a protected area, which shields the colony from winds that can reach 100 mph.
- The female lays a single egg, and the co-operation of both parents is needed if the chick is to survive.
- After the female lays the egg, she transfers it to the feet of the waiting male with as little exposure to the elements as possible.
- The male tends to the egg while the female returns to the sea, both in order to feed and to obtain extra food for feeding her chick when she returns.
- The penguins endure temperatures approaching -80°F and their only source of water is snow that falls on or blows onto the breeding ground.
- When the chicks hatch, the males have only a small meal to feed them, and if the female does not return, they must abandon their chick and return to the sea to feed.
- The parents must then tend to the chick for an additional four months, shuttling back-and-forth to the sea in order to provide food for their young.[2]

---

[2] http://emanuellevy.com/comment/march-of-the-penguins-making-of-an-oscar-docu-6.

Amazing, right? But you're probably still wondering, "What do Penguins have to do with Psalm 8?" When we think of all the amazing things that went into the creation of Emperor Penguins, we should be even more amazed at God's view of us! Namely, God views us in two unique ways, according to this Psalm.

First, God favors us above all other created things. We notice the Psalm is "framed" by praise given to God: "O Lord, our Lord, How majestic is Thy name in all the earth" (verse 1 and verse 9)! But the focal point of the Psalm resides in its middle verses (verses 4-5).

The term "God" in the context of verse five is the Hebrew word, *'elohiym*, which the King James Version of the Bible translates, "angels." And while it is true *'elohiym* in various Old Testament passages can refer to angels and humans alike, the expression, "a little lower than the angels," is not the clear reading of the Hebrew text.[3] A more literal reading of verse 5 is something like this: "But you have caused him to lack *but little of God.*"

In response to the question, "What is so unique about the creation of humans?" an answer of dignity and distinction emerges—in that man is made a little lower than God Himself—crowned

[3] Ronald Allen. *The Majesty of Man* (Portland, Oregon: Multnomah Press, 1984), 71.

by Him with glory and honor. Thus, "It is in the context of the praise of God that man has his true meaning and dignity."[4]

In a truly biblical sense we are not only considered far greater than creation itself, but of greater importance than any other created thing! We carry with us that unique *imago Dei*, which neither angels nor creation possess. We are, in a word, the "apex" of God's creation!

The second thing this Psalm tells us is that we are considered "royalty" (verses 6-9). We need, however, to put the royal perspective of ourselves into proper context. Our royalty is only properly understood in light of the book-end acclamations of the Lord's majesty!

In other words, our royalty is derived from our intimate association with Jesus, the "author and perfecter of our faith" (Hebrews 12:2). For believers, faith in Jesus Christ as Lord and Savior is the sole place of entry into this majestic association with the Creator.

It's important for us to remember what it took for us to have such a position. It's equally important to be reminded of God's original design for male and female—to be crowned with glory and honor and to rule over that which was created. When Adam and Eve

---

[4] Ibid, 71.

rebelled against God, they lost their royal "mantle," as it were, requiring the sacrifice of *Another* to reinstate us.

Romans 5:17 says: "For if by the transgression of the one, death reigned through the one, much more those who receive the abundance of grace and of the gift of righteousness will *reign in life through the One*, Jesus Christ."

Thus, it is only through a direct connection of being "in Christ" we have any possibility of understanding our true value in the eyes of God (verse 6). Today, remember that your royal mantle was bought at an incredible price!

So, penguins may be emperors. Lions may be kings. Firs may be noble. Seas may be great. And mountain ranges majestic. Yet Psalm 8 boldly declares God's favors toward *you*— above all other created things!

20

Agents of God's Love

Gary Derickson, Professor of Biblical Studies, Corban University

Today's Reading: 1 John 4:7-12

Today's Key Verse: "No one has seen God at any time. If we love one another, God abides in us, and His love has been perfected in us" (1 John 4:12 NKJV).

Today's Insights: God has chosen to love His children through His children. God, who cannot be seen by men, makes Himself visible through the loving deeds of His children.

It is when we seek to meet the needs of our brothers and sisters in Christ that God's love fully expresses itself within us and through us ("has been perfected").

Though God could act directly, as He did by sending Jesus, He has chosen to act through us. He has made us the agents through whom He expresses His love.

John is known as the "beloved disciple" and in his Gospel described himself as "the one whom

Jesus loved" four times (John 13:23; 20:2; 21:7, 20). It would be safe to say he was Jesus' favorite. However, being loved so dearly by Jesus did not spoil him, but changed him.

Philip and David Schaff, in their *History of the Christian Church, Vol. 1* (New York: Charles Scribner's Sons, 1910), page 430, report that the church father Jerome described John as "the disciple of love" who, when he became feeble from old age, was carried into the church meetings by his disciples. He would then repeatedly say, "Little Children, love one another." When asked why he kept saying this, he replied, "This is the Lord's command, and if this alone be done, it is enough."

From what John wrote in his First Epistle, we can see he understood fully what Jesus meant when He commanded us to love one another (John 13:34-35).

John's First Epistle can be seen as a reflection or, in some ways, a meditation on Jesus' words in the Upper Room (John 13-16).

That evening, as He anticipated the cross, Jesus faced a very serious problem. He knew what was coming. He also knew that His disciples were still too immature to lead the church following His departure.

Their unpreparedness was blatantly exposed in

their selfish ongoing debate among themselves about who would be the greatest person in Jesus' coming kingdom. In other words, who would hold the highest office in Jesus' coming government? How self-centered were they? They were too arrogant to clean their own feet when entering their host's home, much less anybody else's.

The floor of the room where they dined would have been covered with rugs. Instead of chairs, the table would be provided with couches on which they would lie while eating. Out of courtesy the disciples had bathed before coming. However, they still had to walk through the city's streets.

What did their feet smell like? They smelled like the street. And the street was covered by its own unique kind of dust. It had been the passageway of numerous sheep, goats, donkeys and cows, all who left "presents" behind as they passed through. Those presents turned into the dust that stuck to the disciples' wet feet as they left the bath house and walked to their host's home. Yes, their feet reeked of animal manure.

When they entered their host's home they passed a bowl of water with a towel placed nearby. With no servant present, each would be expected to wash his own feet. None did; though we can expect that Jesus had.

In their world, Rabbis never washed their disciples' feet. Even in a household no one of higher social standing washed the feet of someone socially below them. This hierarchy existed even among the servants. The lowest servant in the household inherited the duty. So, what did Jesus do?

Knowing He was about to die a horrible death, John tells us He *loved* the disciples completely. That love moved Him to action. He took the form of a servant, girding the towel around His waist, and served them. It was then in the context of what Jesus had just done that He commanded them to love one another by following His example of humble servanthood.

After years of meditating on what Jesus did and said that night, John wrote his epistle. Jesus first loved them and then commanded them to follow His pattern in loving one another. Even more significant was His statement that it was in their loving one another that the world would recognize them as Jesus' disciples.

And so, years later John focuses on this same truth when writing his epistle.

Why is it that humbly serving other Christians is so important with God? First, the world cannot see God except through us. That is the point of verse 12.

Second, when we actively love God's children by meeting their needs, we are expressing God's love toward them the way God expresses His love. We are imitating God.

And, just as Jesus promised that the world would recognize our commitment to Him in our attitudes and actions toward each other, so, too, the world will recognize we serve a loving God when we act like Him.

Our invisible God has chosen to reveal Himself to the world through us, the agents of His love. Therefore, let us "love one another" in word and deed today.

21

Who's Sitting at Your Table?

Leroy Goertzen, Associate Professor of Pastoral Theology, Corban University

Today's Reading: Luke 5:27-32

Today's Key Verse: "Jesus answered them, 'It is not the healthy who need a doctor, but the sick. I have not come to call the righteous, but sinners to repentance'" (Luke 5:32 NIV).

Today's Insights: Most cultures around the world place great importance in what happens at the common table beyond the act of eating.

In ancient Mediterranean societies, the culture in which the stories of the Bible were lived out, the table symbolized a place of acceptance, peace, and friendship.

In the Jewish community of the first century, table fellowship was a cultural sensibility that was practiced judiciously and rigorously. In plain words, you don't eat with just anyone! Who you broke bread with indicated who your friends were and where you fit on the social ladder. And so it was in Jesus' day.

The religious leadership had managed in their pursuit of (self) righteousness to separate themselves from the common members of the Jewish community. Many of these were labeled as "sinners"—individuals with whom a common meal would result in impurity.

Ironically, it was amongst these very individuals that Jesus lived and ministered. He was regularly accused of consorting with the social riff-raff of the day—at least so the religious leaders opined as seen in today's reading.

Things could hardly have been messier for Jesus than being the honored guest at a banquet designed to fellowship with "tax collectors and others."

Naturally, Levi, the host, had worldly friends who were on the religious leaders' "do not invite to dinner" list! The question asked by the Pharisees, "Why do you eat and drink with tax collectors and 'sinners'?" highlighted what everyone already knew: Jesus was violating religious and social protocol.

Scott Bartchy writes, "In his message and table praxis, eating with anyone who would eat with him challenged the central role played by table fellowship in reinforcing boundaries and statuses widely believed to be sanctioned by God." Thus, Jesus acted counter-culturally.

Jesus transformed the role of the table from one of preserving ethnic and religious purity to one of announcing grace and acceptance; from enforcing exclusiveness to offering inclusiveness; from marginalizing "sinners" to welcoming them to repentance. This was unprecedented. As a result, he would be misunderstood, suffer undue criticism, and experience alienation and censorship.

Table-fellowship, then, serves as a cultural lens through which to understand Jesus' mission as today's key verse states.

To translate this verse using the table-fellowship metaphor: "It is not the popular and socially apt who need to be invited to eat at our table, but the marginalized ..."

On this, and other occasions, Jesus was enjoying food and fellowship at the table when He announced His salvation. At the table of Zacchaeus, a despised chief tax collector, Jesus spoke grace: "Today salvation has come to this house, because this man, too, is a son of Abraham. For the Son of Man came to seek and to save what was lost" (Luke 19:9-10).

To another marginalized individual, a Roman military man, an astonished Jesus said, "I tell you the truth, I have not found anyone in Israel with such great faith. I say to you that many will come from the east and the west and will take their places at the feast with Abraham, Isaac and Jacob in the kingdom of heaven. But the subjects of the kingdom will be thrown outside, into the darkness, where there will be weeping and gnashing of teeth" (Matt 8:10-12).

Here, Jesus announced a stunning reversal: hated outsiders like gentile Romans from the west would be invited to sit at the table with the Jewish Patriarchs while Jewish religious leaders and other entitled insiders would be shown the door. Jesus explains in Luke's parallel passage: "Indeed there are those who are last who will be first, and the first who will be last" (13:29).

Christians must catch the vision of Jesus' inclusive welcoming presence amongst "sinners" where God's transforming grace can be shared in word and deed. Eddie Gibbs writes, "Hospitality entails not only a seat in the church, but a place at the table. The missional church is one that welcomes all comers, regardless of their lifestyle and beliefs, but always with a view to their radical transformation."

With whom have you broken bread recently? Who do you feel comfortable with inviting to your table? Could Jesus bring His friends and social acquaintances? Your answer will reveal whether your table is a place of transforming grace or a place of intractable indifference.

22

God's Timing

Sheldon C. Nord, President
Corban University

Today's Reading: Genesis 22:1-18

Today's Key Verse: "And so after waiting patiently, Abraham received what was promised" (Hebrews 6:15 NIV).

Today's Insights: Abraham has gone through history known as a great man of faith. More significantly, he is known as *The* Man of Faith.

Christians today revere Abraham for the way he lived in utter dependence on and complete trust in the Lord. It wasn't just one instance that prompted him to be forever known as The Man of Faith, but rather multiple instances and, most importantly, the way Abraham lived his everyday life.

Our reading in Genesis 22 takes us through the well-known story where God tested Abraham by asking him to sacrifice his son, Isaac. Abraham loved his son very much, and if it were me I would have felt shocked, bewildered and perhaps even betrayed by God. "Why would he give me the gift of a son and then take him away from me like this?"

We don't get a glimpse into Abraham's feelings, however, in the Scripture. We only see that he obeyed. And whatever he was thinking and feeling as he drew his knife is kept from us as well. All we see from our reading is that God stepped in by sending an angel at the last possible moment to prevent Abraham from killing his son. *In the nick of time* God stepped in.

Prior to this is another Abraham story with which we are familiar. It is the story of God's promise that Abraham would be the father of many nations. This happened when Abraham was 75 years old, at the time God called him to leave his country and go to the land God would show him.

Fifteen years later, when Abraham was 90, God renewed his promise. And ten years later, when Abraham was 100, he and Sarah finally had their son. What stands out here? The extremely slow passage of time.

Scripture doesn't emphasize it, but the truth is that Abraham didn't hear the Lord's promise on one day, sleep on it and then wake up the next day to the fulfillment of that promise. He had to wait. And wait. And wait. Twenty-five years passed before Isaac was born.

What do you think Abraham was doing all that time? I think he was living life, faithfully going about his duties and honoring God in his daily interactions with the people in his life. I don't think he stressed out about how much time was passing because what we know from today's key verse is that Abraham waited *patiently*.

These two stories about Abraham reveal God's oh-so-interesting timing. From the point of testing to being in physical position to slay his son, Abraham and Isaac were saved when God intervened in the last possible moment. From the promise of a son to the birth of his son, Abraham had to wait twenty-five years. The second story makes us think that God holds time so loosely that he doesn't really care whether a year or 25 years pass. Meanwhile, the first story reveals that God is in every moment, down to the millisecond.

From our human perspective we often cannot make sense of God's timing. I was 27 years old when I married Jamie, and I had been praying for years for that Proverbs 31 woman. Today I praise God for his perfect timing in bringing me my wife. There are other instances now that challenge me every day to wait just as Hebrews 6:15 tells us Abraham waited—patiently.

Psalm 18 tells us, "As for God, his way is perfect." There is no room for us to contest God, to challenge Him or berate Him for being "late," for operating on a time schedule that is drastically different from the one we want. And if we're honest with ourselves, the one we want is a direct result of our on-demand, fast-food, smartphone, Google-at-our-fingertips culture.

The truth is that the God who created time is always in control. He moves in mighty ways, whether that means we wait on Him for many, many years, or He instantaneously intervenes when we least expect it.

23

What Is Love?

Ron Marrs, Kairos Program Director
Corban University

Today's Reading: 1 John 4:7-11

Today's Key Verse: "This is love: not that we loved God, but he loved and sent his Son as an atoning sacrifice for our sins. Dear friends, since God so loved us, we also ought to love one another" (1 John 4:10-11 NIV).

Today's Insights: The apostle John instructs Christ followers in this passage to love one another as God loves us. How has God loved us? He used His resource to take the initiative to sacrificially meet our need.

What resource did the Father have that He used to love us? The passage tells us that the resource was the Son whom the Father sent as an atoning sacrifice. This would suggest that in our endeavor to love we need to analyze the resources at our disposal to meet the needs of others.

I heard a pastor at a mission conference tell the story of a North American Christian who went to a Bible conference in Africa. At the end of this conference a pastor stood a dozen or so young people up in front of the people gathered there and said, "We are going to take up a collection to provide for these young people to go over the mountains to take the gospel to our neighbors. Please give what you are able to give so that we can send them."

These African Christians didn't have many possessions. Some women had two dresses and they began a pile of extra dresses which would be sold to send the young people out. Some men had one pair of shoes and they began to add to the pile their only pair of shoes.

After this had gone on for a time, the observer noticed the people crying and asked why they were crying. His host said, "They are crying because they don't have any more to give."

I have often thought about this story because frequently Christians in the United States get tired of being asked to give to the Lord's work. I've not heard any stories of people here crying because they didn't have anything more to give.

We have so many resources to give to meet the needs of others: money, time, a listening ear, our presence, our energy, and more. The first step of love is to examine what resources we have to meet the needs of others.

God's love is sacrificial. The precious Son of God died on the cross for our sins—the supreme sacrifice. This love was shown by a missionary, Bruce Olson, as described in the book *Bruchko*.

When an eye infection was raging in the South American tribe he was trying to reach with the gospel, Olson grew deeply frustrated. He had an ointment that would clear up the infection. The people, however, would not use it. So, Olson touched an infected eye and then touched his own eye.

When Olson got the infection, he put the ointment on his own eye in the presence of the people to show them its healing nature. He gave the ointment to leaders in the tribe so that they could dispense the medicine.

I'm not sure I would have thought of that or wanted to sacrifice my well-being in this way, but Olson did and showed love to these people by meeting a need.

And finally, God's love meets the needs of others. In the passage today we are told that the need we had was for forgiveness of sins, and that the atoning sacrifice on the cross accomplished this.

I had a wonderful mentor in seminary, Loren Fischer. He started me on my journey to articulate the needs of people and how God and His church are to meet those needs.

There are at least 13 needs of people that can be supported scripturally. Among them are these needs: People have physical needs, therefore we provide physical care. People need trust, therefore we point them to the only one worthy of unqualified trust, God, and we seek to be trustworthy people. People need purpose, therefore we provide meaningful involvement. People need hope, therefore we provide precious certainties from God's Word. People need truth, therefore we teach God's Word. We need to be alert to the needs of the people around us.

So, use your resources to take the initiative to sacrificially meet the needs of others. And what will keep you going in this endeavor? It's this: Remember the love of God which compels you and me to love others (2 Corinthians 5:14-15).

24

Deliverance *In* or *From?*

Brenda Roth, Vice President for Student Life, Corban University

Today's Reading: Isaiah 43:1-21

Today's Key Verses: "Forget the former things; do not dwell on the past. See, I am doing a new thing! Now it springs up; do you not perceive it? I am making a way in the wilderness and streams in the wasteland" (Isaiah 43:18-19 NIV).

Today's Insights: As faithful believers, we know that trials are part of the Christian life. We know that testing helps us to become mature and complete (James 1) and offers a rich opportunity to exemplify the richness of life in Jesus Christ (2 Corinthians 4).

At the same time, however, we would all probably agree that spiritual desert-wandering can be fatiguing, confusing, and discouraging.

A recent stint in the desert caused me to realize that although I've rightly been focused on deliverance in times past, I've also frequently confused deliverance *in* with deliverance *from*. Let me explain.

In most of my trips to the desert, I've focused on finding my way out. I've sometimes wrestled with a willingness to admit that I'm even *in* a desert at first. But once I've admitted that I'm there, and have embraced that there are good things for me to interact with during my visit, I've also been sure that at some point God's delivering hand will extricate me.

During this recent desert visit, I dove into my Bible and, in hindsight, realized I'd gravitated toward passages that fell into three different categories: those that talked about accepting the desert, those that talked about benefitting from what was within the desert, and those that talked about deliverance.

The passages that challenged me to adopt an attitude of acceptance included James 1, Isaiah 43, Isaiah 40 and 2 Corinthians 4. Passages that exhorted me to actively engage with what I encountered in the desert included Genesis 22, Matthew 11, Ephesians 3, 5 and 6, Galatians 5, and Philippians 1 and 4. I spent days and weeks exploring these rich passages. I encourage you to do some exploring yourself!

Passages from the book of Hebrews, however, redirected my conception of deliverance and these are what I want to direct your attention to right now.

Hebrews 2 challenged me to be careful to not miss the purpose of my desert experience and reminded me that without mindfulness, my attention tends to drift. Hebrews 5 and 6 urged me to submit, grow up, and pursue maturity. And Hebrews 9 and 10 sobered me with reminders about Christ's blood paying a ransom that freed me from captivity. Deep and challenging passages to be sure, and what I expected. Then I arrived at Hebrews 11 ...

The Hebrews 11 heroes of the faith, these witnesses who also travelled through spiritual deserts, found the deliverance I was craving. In reading this passage carefully, however, I realized that what they had acquired was not a deliverance *from*. It was a deliverance *in*.

Hebrews 11:13 says, "they did not receive the things promised; they only saw them and welcomed them from a distance," and 11:39 says, "these were all commended for their faith, yet none of them received what had been promised." As these heroes of the faith wrestled with the challenges before them, they somehow found deliverance while not yet actually being delivered. These heroes did not see deliverance, but they considered themselves to be delivered. They were delivered *in*, but not *from*.

Through this experience I have learned that deliverance *from* is about the disappearance of challenging circumstances.

In contrast, deliverance *in* is about locating deep peace, joy, and fruitfulness while still in the midst of pain: "being sure of what we hope for and certain of what we do not see" (11:1).

Isaiah 43 is the passage that got my attention in the first place, but as I went back and read it again, once-subtle messages emphasizing deliverance *in* became much clearer to me. Check out verse 19:

- I am *doing* a new thing
- *Now* it springs up
- I am *making* a way in the wilderness and streams in the wasteland

These present tense statements tell me that deliverance is a here-and-now gift that can only be realized if I am willing to accept it in the here-and-now.

Yearning for deliverance *from* is not bad and there are plenty of Scripture passages and Bible stories that provide us with this as an appropriate model.

Then again, failing to grasp deliverance *in* as one of God's gifts is to miss a unique beauty that cannot be known in any other context.

My desert? I think I might still be in it. But I don't really care because it's beautiful here.

25

Editing Jesus?

Marty Trammell, Chair of Humanities
Corban University

Today's Reading: Ephesians 4:1-32.

Today's Key Verse: "Therefore each of you must put off falsehood and speak truthfully to your neighbor, for we are all members of one body" (Ephesians 4:25 NIV).

Today's Insight: Sometimes we edit Jesus out of the story of His life in us. Here's one way to make *Him* the main character again.

In talking to a friend who is a videographer, I learned that editing video takes 10 hours for every 1 hour of recorded material. That made me think about how time-intensive editing is. It also made me think about the time and energy I spend editing the movie of *my* life.

I know God has said that "all things work together for good" (Romans 8:28), but I still find it less humiliating to cut out the raw footage that reveals my weaknesses—to put some spin on my sin. I'm more comfortable deleting the ugly parts of my story and dragging them to the trash bin. After all, no respectable person needs to see how much I am in need of a Savior!

I've found, too, that those who do not yet believe in God can tell when I do this. It's obvious to them that I've purchased, at a very high price, some well-packaged evangelically-approved editing software from a Christian bookstore. Regrettably, using a little chroma key to "sweeten" the re-telling of *my* life is why they label *all* Christians "hypocrites."

In juxtaposition to Moses who, according to Paul, continued to wear a veil over his face so that the children of God would not see the fading of the Old Covenant (2 Corinthians 3:13), many of us wear a veil that hides the glory of the New. We hide how the shining righteousness of Christ continues to transform our struggles and sin, and we replace the mysteries of His grace with images made from ... well, carefully arranged pixels.

Like us, unbelievers would like to see human lives re-created, not re-touched. Even new believers long to see lives authentically and beautifully changed by the God they've just experienced—the God who they already know does not appreciate forgeries in His gallery.

Still, like Ibsen's family of photographers in *The Wild Duck*, we often find ourselves blinded by a "life lie" that makes retouching photographs and editing video a religiously responsible occupation—something we learn to do as we "mature" in the faith.

It seems so strange that even though the Spirit told us that Jesus' strength is "made perfect in weakness" (2 Corinthians 12:9), and that pretending we're "without sin" makes us "liars" (1 John 1:8), and that we must "put off falsehood" (Ephesians 4:25), we still find clever excuses to edit the errors and paint over the pain. Is it because we think faking our story will produce more glory? Is it because we've been hurt by the condemnation of our Christian brothers and sisters?

If we truly believe that we should "put off falsehood and speak truthfully," shouldn't we stop splicing out the realness in our humanity and destroying the beautiful art in the unfinished masterpiece our Creator calls Redemption?

OK. I should stop right here. I probably need to edit this a bit, before someone reads it and gets the idea that some of us still need a Savior.

26

Being in the Right Place

Greg Trull, Dean, School of Ministry
Corban University

Today's Reading: Hebrews 10:11-14

Today's Key Verse: "Day after day every priest stands and performs his religious duties; again and again he offers the same sacrifices, which can never take away sins. But when this priest, Jesus, had offered for all time one sacrifice for sins, he sat down at the right hand of God" (Hebrews 10:11-12 NIV).

Today's Insights: God's grand sense of irony showed as soon as we entered the hall. Our first Corban graduation in Cameroon would begin soon. After looking at several venues, the local planning team chose this hall and decorated it beautifully. The Lord had arranged it so that we would graduate in the same hall where we started years before. Corban's representatives would even sit in the very same place we did on our first day! Three years after the pioneering African pastor group began our training program, they would now graduate.

Sitting in this hall in these seats, we were witnessing a work completed by God. A display of His power and grace. In a much greater way, when believers see Jesus Christ seated at the right hand of the Father, we see an eternal display of power and grace.

The Lord displayed His power when He sat down after His sacrifice. The passage paints a striking contrast between the work of the Levitical priests and Jesus our High Priest. It says of the Levites that "day after day" they stood to offer "again and again" sacrifices that "could never take away sin" (10:11). They had to keep offering those sacrifices because the sacrifices never really worked. They were roofers that came every week, but never really fixed the leak. Their continuation of work only demonstrated its futility.

Jesus, on the other hand, did His work wholly. He offered "one sacrifice" for "all time" and "made perfect forever" His followers (10:12). Then, while the other priests stood again, He sat down. His position today shows us His power to totally defeat sin and eternally secure salvation. No more work is needed. No one, not even we ourselves, can complete God's salvation. It is finished.

Jesus' exalted position at the right hand of the Father also displays God's grace to us. Jesus entered into heaven on our behalf (Hebrews 9:24). Because He sits next to the Father for us, we have confidence and full assurance that we have complete access to the eternal God (10:19-21). No priest, no medium, not even a pastor is required to access the Lord on our behalf. Because Jesus is already there, we can come at any time. Here we find grace and help in times of our greatest need (Hebrews 4:16).

Corban professors enjoying graduation from the very seats of the first day of class showed God's goodness. He had finished a work He had led us to. Jesus sitting in His place at this time reminds us that He has secured total victory. And that victory is ours.

Leaders Are All Ears

P. Griffith Lindell, Dean,
Hoff School of Business
Corban University

Today's Reading: Proverbs 18:2-15

Today's Key Verse: "Wise men and women are always learning, always listening for fresh insights" (Proverbs 18:15 MSG).

Today's Insights: People who are wise are good listeners. This skill of listening well takes a certain intentionality. Effective leaders have learned that art. In a January 2001 article in Harvard Business Review, Jim Collins introduced the world to the "Level 5 Leadership" and HBR declared that "The Triumph of Humility and Fierce Resolve" change the workplace for good.

Those who practice humility listen actively. Active listening is a skill not easily developed. The goal must always be mutual understanding.

That discipline of humility demands of the believer a spiritual commitment that includes meditating on God's Word, prayer, and an awareness of the need to moderate our strengths when under stress. This listening takes discipline, a willingness to be open to learning, and a commitment to grow. If you build a team around you that's willing to help each other grow, the yield is a certain freedom to listen, respond, change and grow. Sometimes, though, the situations that bring the "worst" out of you are not clear, moral choices. Instead, they are ambiguous.

I asked one of my mentors years ago why he had not engaged in an exchange with a client about the facts of a situation. His answer shocked me. "I don't need to let him know that I know more about it than he does; I just need to let him know that I'm listening to him and understanding his perspective."

That was a revelation to me. I was raised to stand for "the truth" of a situation—despite who was expounding. My mentor practiced a humble spirit because it was about the client, not him. Arrogance, I learned, was all about me—proving what I knew—and that mentor taught me that, even at its best, trying to be the *smartest one in the room* is dishonest: no one knows everything.

The key to effective listening is mentioned in our key verse: asking good questions. Good questions are not simply a matter of casual probing. These questions take forethought—

that's a key. Before the conversation. Not during. Preparing for a learning conversation is not a casual endeavor. That preparation sometimes involves your time to think about the attributes or issues around a scheduled topic of conversation. Skill to develop a conversation that achieves understanding of the issues involved will develop knowledge.

Knowledge. Always learning, looking for more. Filling our minds with facts, concepts and diligently connecting the dots. The acquiring of this learning we most often associate with the mind, not the heart. Heart knowledge changes the meaning here. Ignorance rears its ugly head often from those who have the conceit of head knowledge. That conceit is the result of lots of learning, but to no good purpose.

What we know is only as good as how we love. "By your love people will know that you are my disciples," Jesus told us. The head that gathers much "knowledge" without the heart being impacted breeds the "mistress to pride," as one commentator put it.

That started in the beginning. Mankind, tempted by the evil one with "knowledge," quickly took the bait. To be like God himself ... what a rush. But think about it: God had already given them what they needed to survive and do quite well in the world created for them. Why want more? Sure the tree's fruit might have looked enticing—but that was not the temptation.

This was the first attack: Be like God. The result? Knowledge without love. We cannot be "wholly like God" for God is Love. Our knowledge—head or heart—suffers from our imitation of God without the love of God. Knowing "good from evil" is not merely cognitive activity.

Life-long learning. Prudent learning. We need God's Word to teach us not only how to walk in "the light of God's presence," but also, even more importantly, how to develop a single-mindedness in our approach to learning. Wise, discerning hearts must change who we are in the way we live. It must open up our minds and hearts to new insights—the freshness of allowing God to teach us more about what we are learning.

Are you listening? Asking good questions? Or just talking?

28

What Is the Mark of Great Commission Success?

Kevin Brubaker, Vice President for Business, Corban University

Today's Reading: Matthew 28:1-20

Today's Key Verse: "Therefore go and make disciples of all nations, baptizing them in the name of the Father and of the Son and of the Holy Spirit, and teaching them to obey everything I have commanded you. And surely I am with you always, to the very end of the age" (Matthew 28:19-20 NIV).

Today's Insights: It is possible to get lost in the details of the Great Commission. Look at the action words: "go" (literally "going"), "make disciples," "teaching," "baptizing." What is the main point of this passage?

While four terms could be construed as commands, there is only one imperative: "make disciples." All of the other words are a means to the end product: a disciple.

It is important to go, it is important to teach, it is important to baptize, but all are done with the end goal in sight.

The heart of the Great Commission is to make disciples. If we go but do nothing else, we fail. If we teach but don't do it for the purpose of making disciples, we fail. If we evangelize and convert souls and baptize them but do not assist them in spiritual growth, we fail.

We live and minister in different environments. In some places in the world, you will do well to have one or two disciples for a lifetime of ministry. In other places, one hundred or two hundred disciples is attainable.

In the end, each of us will be judged by how well we pursued the command of making disciples. Above everything else you and I do, the Lord wants this one thing done well!

29

Fighting Our Battles

Sheldon C. Nord, President
Corban University

Today's Reading: Psalm 18

Today's Key Verse: "For our struggle is not against flesh and blood, but against the rulers, against the authorities, against the powers of this dark world and against the spiritual forces of evil in the heavenly realms" (Ephesians 6:12 NIV).

Today's Insights: Unless you're in the military, you're not likely to do much by way of fighting literal battles these days. Though we may not actually be standing on a battlefield, we can still relate when we read this Psalm by David. How is that? It's because the brutality of a battle and the fear induced by the enemy are not unique to war. The parallels between physical battles in war and the internal battles we fight on a personal level are numerous.

Here are a few words and phrases in our reading today that we can all relate to, even when we're not fighting a physical battle: distress, cried to God, tremble, trample, lose heart, torrents of destruction overwhelmed me, rescue, support, armed me with strength, scale a wall, and victory, to name a few.

I have felt all these things in the various trials and triumphs in my life. Though I'm not actually at war I will have an enemy, allies, armor to put on and obstacles to overcome. I will experience the same torrent of emotions that a warrior has: fear, anxiety and dread, as well as hope, confidence and pride. We experience each of these in the face of trials and challenges.

I remember pursuing my Ph.D. in higher education at Indiana University. It was an exciting time in my life, being immersed in a field and discipline that held my keen interest. But the road was far from smooth. I faced many challenges and at times discouragement. I stayed the course and earned my degree, but not without regular trips to the foot of the cross. I continually sought clarity from God and affirmation that I needed to persist.

In the end we cannot turn to our circumstances for relief, nor to our friends and family. They can cheer us on, which we appreciate, but we are left longing for more ... for divine intervention. We are reminded of our sheer dependence on the Lord God in all His sovereignty.

Though our modern day civilian battles are not

waged on the battlefield, they are just as intense. Our key verse today shares the truth that our struggles involve Satan, and that spiritual forces are firing on all four cylinders when we're in a battle—whether it involves people or is within ourselves.

Praise the Lord, He equips us!

He gives us armor to wear (Ephesians 6:10-18) so that we are not defenseless in the attack. He gives us the Counselor (John 14:16-17) to speak His truth and guide us. He gives us His Word, our offensive weapon against the enemy (Ephesians 6:17). He gives us His promise that He will never leave or forsake us (Deuteronomy 31:6). And He gives us His overwhelming peace (Philippians 4:7).

No matter how great or overwhelming our struggles, we are not defenseless. We serve a victorious God who has defeated Satan and who delights in us, equipping us for each and every battle we encounter.

30

Crossroads

Pam Teschner, Associate Provost of Academics, Corban University

Today's Reading: Ephesians 4:25-32

Today's Key Verse: "Get rid of all bitterness, rage and anger, brawling and slander, along with every form of malice" (Ephesians 4:31 NIV).

Today's Insights: None of us pass through this life unscathed. At some point, we will be pierced by wrong and stand at a crossroads. The course of our lives will be set by what we choose at that critical juncture.

Two paths diverge and lead in very different directions with very different destinations. The cross stands dead center in the path of forgiveness. The pilgrim of forgiveness embraces the cross and finds healing and freedom. But the road of resentment leads to captivity and hardness. The insidious root of bitterness bores into the spirit and contorts the countenance. It sends its deadly tendrils into every crevice of the heart and bleeds it dry.

I have stood before a crossroads of deep hurt, and struggled taking the first steps. The cross loomed ahead, and soon I stood eye level with the bloody feet of Jesus. Looking up the length of His brutalized body, I saw the ravages of sin. He became every wrong, every obscenity of humanity and every heinous crime. Then He paid the debt with His life. There is no sin so great that He will not forgive.

Human nature screams retribution, but the Spirit of God whispers forgiveness. Our humanness hangs on to the hurt and drags around the dead body of the past. Eventually we become chained to the past and cannot grasp the future.

Forgiveness breaks the chains and frees the soul. It is not a feeling but a choice of obedience. It does not wait for apologies or repentance and is not contingent upon sincerity. It embraces the one who wronged us with the forgiveness of Jesus Christ.

Forgiveness does not change the past, erase the consequences of bad choices, or always repair broken relationships. It does not minimize the hurt or stop the pain, but it lays the aching heart and broken pieces in the wounded hands of Jesus and trusts Him to do a healing work.

I have learned that forgiveness is a long journey of giving the wrong and the hurt to

God ... again and again and ever again.

Some time ago, I ran across a little red notebook I had tucked away. I knew it was time to let go of the penned past, and burn pages and pages of awful memories.

With the heat of the fire warming my face, I watched memories turn to black ash. A sense of finality and freedom settled into my soul as the fire died. In time, a crown of beauty and blessing rose from the ashes.

There comes a time when we must purge the memories of the past to find the freedom of the present and grasp the goodness of the future.

31

People of Hope

Jim Hills, Professor of Humanities
Corban University

Today's Reading: John 14:1-6

Today's Key Verse: "And if I go and prepare a place for you, I will come again, and receive you unto myself; that where I am, there ye may be also" (John 14:3 KJV).

Today's Insights: It was an amazing sight. A huge man wearing a sweat-soaked wrestling singlet turned a cartwheel. Then a somersault. He rolled up onto his big feet and grinned.

The reason for this unlikely gymnastics display was amazing, too. Rulon Gardner, a farmer from Wyoming, had just defeated Alexander Karelin, the greatest Greco-Roman wrestler the world has ever seen.

Karelin, 285 pounds of skill and muscle, was considered unbeatable. To increase stamina he went on long runs through knee-deep Siberian snow. Even for a big man he was so freakishly strong he frightened the big, tough men who had to compete against him. He often simply yanked them off the wrestling mat and slammed them down as if they were no more than a rolled-up rug or a sack of rice. He was unbeaten in a decade and a half, and had given up two points—yes, two points—in five years.

But now the great Karelin stood at the edge of the mat in silence, blinking slowly, apparently as dumbfounded as the arena full of wrestling fans who had calculated the possibility of this defeat at about the same odds as ice on the Amazon.

But if Rulon Gardner was surprised, he didn't show it. He had thought all along he could win, he said. "I trained hard," he told sportscaster Jim Gray.

This, it seemed to me, was a striking example of hope: desire combined with expectation. Rulon Gardner had not trained hour upon hour, day after day, week after week, month upon month, expecting to lose. His desire was Olympic gold, and he knew what he needed to do to bring back the medal.

This was no idle fantasy, no mere daydream. He didn't just show up in Sydney and indulge in wishful thinking. He came in the confidence born of disciplined preparation and astute strategy. He would use his size and farmer's strength—he'd been moving stubborn cows for a long time, he explained—to wear his opponents down. And he did.

Desire combined with expectation and resulting in action: this will do as a description of the classic Christian virtue of hope.

For the Christian, hope is bound up with faith. Abraham, spoken of as a great example of faith, one who "believed God" and was accounted righteous, left his home in Ur because he wanted something better. "I will make of you a great nation," God told him, and Abraham believed Him.

But Abraham had to do something, too. His hope was not inert. He packed up his goods, said goodbye to his prosperous and uneventful life in Ur, organized his family and servants into a caravan, and "went out."

To some, this must have seemed a terribly risky enterprise. Why would anyone abandon comfortable circumstances and head out into the wilderness, into the unknown?

Because of hope. God had given Abraham the desire for something better, and Abraham was confident that God would honor His promise. So out he went, with his camels and goats and at least one nephew and his family, out into the dust and heat—and out of comfortable obscurity into his great place in history, as, all along, he knew he would.

The apostle Paul, too, was a man of hope. He

worked hard, confident that his labor would not be in vain. "I planted," he said to the Corinthian believers. "Apollos watered, but God gave the increase."

We, too, look forward with anticipation and expectation to the fulfillment of the promise that illuminates our lives. At dinner nearly two thousand years ago Jesus promised His disciples, "I go to prepare a place for you. And if I go and prepare a place for you, I will come again, and receive you unto myself; that where I am, there ye may be also."

Not long afterward, Luke tells us, these men saw the first part of that promise fulfilled: "While they beheld, he was taken up; and a cloud received Him out of their sight." And two men in white reminded those astonished onlookers, "This same Jesus, which is taken up from you into heaven, shall so come in like manner as ye have seen him go into heaven."

We people of hope look forward to this great event. We desire it. We expect it. Even so come, Lord Jesus.

32

Failure Is Not Final With Jesus

Mark A. Jacobson, Associate Professor of Theology, Corban University

Today's Reading: John 21:1-17

Today's Key Verse: "Feed my sheep!" (John 21:17 LEB).

Today's Insights: The point of the narrative of Jesus' seaside breakfast with Peter and a few other disciples, most notably the other two forming the inner circle—James and John, has often been missed.

A popular take on Jesus' three-fold "Do you love me?" and Peter's "You know that I love you!" makes a big point about Jesus changing the word for "love" in the third, and climactic, question from the verb *agapaō* to the more common, "lesser" word for love, *phileō*. That's because with his denial of his Lord fresh on his mind, Peter could only manage to affirm his love for Jesus each time with nothing more than *phileō*.

Then, according to how this explanation goes, when Jesus asks Peter for the third time, "Do you love me?" Jesus uses *phileō* instead of *agapaō*, as if to say, "Peter, I know you don't love me with an *agape* kind of love; do you love me even as family or friend?" That's why, so it goes, Peter was grieved. But none of this is to John's point as he tells us this story.

Yes, Peter's grief can be connected directly to the memory of his denial of Jesus; yes, Peter had reason to grieve after Jesus asked the question for the third time. But Peter's grief had nothing to do with the use of a lesser word for love.

For one thing, John enjoys variety in the choice of his words. In his report of Jesus' three questions, John alternates between two words for tending sheep ("feed" in #1 and #3; "shepherd" in #2), two words for sheep ("lambs" in #1; "sheep" in #2 and #3) and, yes, two words for love.

That we should not make more of these two words for love is indicated by the fact that in regard to the familiar expression "the disciple whom Jesus loved," in 20:2 John uses the verb *phileō* while here in this context he uses *agapaō* (21:7). Besides this, Jesus most likely was speaking Aramaic with His disciples, not Greek.

The point of this narrative is simpler and more powerful. After Peter's denial of Jesus, his leadership of the disciples, which, if we can read between the lines, never went uncontested by the others, must have been held in question. Peter himself had doubts; who wouldn't have given his same failure?

The reason that Peter was so grieved after the third question was because Jesus was reminding him, in front of the others, of his three-fold denial. But this wasn't to humiliate Peter; it was to reinstate him to the leadership role that Jesus had assigned to him: "Feed my sheep!" Not once did Jesus say this; He repeated it twice more, and He did it in front of the other disciples. Jesus was intentionally reinstating Peter as leader. Peter denied the Lord three times; Jesus tells him three times to feed His sheep.

Failure is not final with Jesus; that's the point of this narrative.

We may think, because of failures on our part similar to that of Peter, that Jesus is through with us, that we have no use thinking that we can serve the Lord in a leadership position.

I identify with this; every pastor and church leader does. We are painfully aware of our own personal denials of Jesus Christ. Why would the Lord ever use us in His ministry? But He does, in spite of our failures and shortcomings. In fact, as did Peter, we learn from them; we grow stronger because of them.

For all of us who serve the Lord, the grace of God in forgiving our sins becomes a powerful motivation to give our lives fully for whatever He calls us to do.

33

A Case of Missionary Malpractice!

Paul E. Johnson, Assistant Professor of Intercultural Studies, Corban University

Today's Reading: Jonah 3-4

Today's Key Verses: "But it displeased Jonah exceedingly, and he was angry. And he prayed to the LORD and said, 'O LORD, is not this what I said when I was yet in my country? That is why I made haste to flee to Tarshish; for I knew that you are a gracious God and merciful, slow to anger and abounding in steadfast love, and relenting from disaster. Therefore now, O LORD, please take my life from me, for it is better for me to die than to live'" (Jonah 4:1-3 ESV).

Today's Insights: Jonah was angry at God! His greatest fear had been realized–God had relented from destroying Israel's arch-enemies, the Assyrians, causing Jonah great personal disgrace. God used His reluctant prophet's message of calamity to cause the Ninevites to believe God and repent of their evil ways.

Why was Nineveh's salvation considered a disaster for Jonah? From Jonah's perspective, God's display of compassion and mercy toward Nineveh jeopardized His exclusive covenant with Israel. Jonah believed that God's character (mercy, compassion, forgiveness) and covenant blessings were intended for Israel alone. God had revealed His gracious character and renewed His covenant with the Israelites following their rebellion with the Golden Calf (Exodus 34:6-10).

Jonah believed that God's covenant was made with Israel alone, not the Gentile nations who deserve judgment (Exodus 34:10-17). Jonah likely knew God had promised to use the Assyrians to destroy Israel and take her into exile (Amos 5:27, Hosea 11:5). Israel fell to Assyria 37 years later (722 B.C.).

Jonah had fled toward Tarshish because he knew that God was compassionate and slow to anger. When God relented from bring calamity on Nineveh, Jonah exploded in intense anger and traveled east of the city, where he built a shelter and enjoyed the shade of a rapid-growing plant.

Jonah may have thought that God would still bring judgment upon Nineveh. He couldn't imagine that God would not judge the evil city and was happy to wait to see if God would follow-through with His threat of judgment.

Jonah's attitude symbolized the self-absorbed Jewish nation, enjoying the blessings of God's covenant while refusing to share His gracious and kind character with the nations.

In chapter 1, God judged Jonah's disobedience and lack of compassion through a great storm and fish.

In chapter 4, God intervened in Jonah's self-absorbed sulking with a simple worm and an oppressive wind. Jonah is greatly discomforted, first by God's gracious response to Nineveh's repentance and then by the loss of shade from the sweltering sun and scorching wind. He had been overjoyed for his own temporary comfort but not for the Ninevites' salvation. Because God had displayed His character-driven compassion to an evil enemy of Israel, Jonah lost all reason for living (4:3).

Jonah 4:9-11 says, "But God said to Jonah, 'Do you do well to be angry for the plant?' And he said, 'Yes, I do well to be angry, angry enough to die.' And the Lord said, 'You pity the plant, for which you did not labor, nor did you make it grow, which came into being in a night and perished in a night. And should not I pity Nineveh, that great city, in which there are more than 120,000 persons who do not know their right hand from their left, and also much cattle?'"

God wanted Jonah—and Israel—to see the contradiction between His display of grace and compassion on Nineveh (and Jonah), and Jonah's complete lack of concern for the eternal destiny of the Ninevites. Jonah, in his self-absorbed devotion, believed God's covenant blessings insulated them from involvement with Gentile nations.

God wanted Jonah to realize he had no right to be angry over Nineveh or the plant. He had not given life to or sustained either of them. Jonah, like Israel, cared more for his personal well-being and covenant blessing than for the spiritual destiny of hundreds of thousands of people.

Jonah depicted a tragic example of the self-focused nation of Israel. Both Jonah and disobedient Israel had created their own understanding of God's will that revolved around their own comfort, success and well-being. Jonah had disconnected God's covenant relationship and blessings on Israel from God's concern and compassion for lost Gentile peoples.

Both were guilty before God of disobedience, self-centeredness and disaffection. While clinging to their covenant with God, Jonah and Israel had lost the capacity to reflect God's character and will toward others. By contrast, God desired that His gracious nature and character be proclaimed to the great city of Nineveh filled with people who desperately needed to know Him!

What about you in your relationship with the Lord? Do you feel a subtle cultural pressure to keep your faith in Jesus Christ to yourself so as to not appear "intolerant" toward others?

Is your knowledge of Jesus and His character (gracious, compassionate, slow to anger, abundant in loving kindness) evident in your words and life?

Do you see others as obstacles or objects of God's love? Do you gladly respond of people without Jesus Christ with compassion and kindness?

Let us strive to live for Jesus Christ by living like Christ in the world! "For the love of Christ compels us" (2 Corinthians 5:14).

34

What in Heaven Is God Doing?

E. Allen Jones III, Assistant Professor of Bible, Corban University

Today's Reading: 2 Peter 3:3-13

Today's Key Verse: "But do not forget this one thing, dear friends: With the Lord a day is like a thousand years, and a thousand years are like a day. The Lord is not slow in keeping his promise, as some understand slowness. He is patient with you, not wanting anyone to perish, but everyone to come to repentance" (2 Peter 3:8-9 NIV).

Today's Insights: A government cracks down on an unregistered church—we cry out, "Injustice!" A mother in Paris weeps over her son—why does terror spread? The global economy crumbles—a protestor shouts, "Occupy!" A friend betrays—where is love and honor? Humanity decays—we cry, we weep, we shout, "God, what are you doing? What in heaven are you doing?"

Daily, we face sin and its effects in the world. We suffer, and we wonder what God is doing.

We have heard, "Patience–God will deal with wickedness. Only, we must wait on His timing," but, perhaps, there is another way to hear the apostle's words. Perhaps there is a call to see from God's perspective as we seek to think His thoughts after Him.

When wickedness festers and spreads in human hearts—not mere frailty in a broken world, but intentional and active evil—the righteous rightly ask why God allows such things. Even the wicked have considered the matter. Peter tells us, the wicked say, "Where is this 'coming' he promised? Ever since our fathers died, everything goes on as it has since the beginning of creation" (verse 4). They have worked out the arithmetic and found God wanting. Like a lenient parent, He has threatened judgment for sin, but He will not follow through.

As believers, do we secretly agree? Do we cry out to God to remind Him of His duty? If God is not an incompetent parent, perhaps He has dozed on his watch. Perhaps He does not see how bad His world has become? Perhaps He needs us to call Him to action? Put so bluntly, we reject these thoughts, but let us not fear the question and its answer. In this passage, our bold questions receive striking answers.

First, Peter confirms that there will be judgment. "The present heavens and earth are reserved for fire, being kept for the day of judgment and destruction of ungodly men" (verse 7). The wicked carry on by "deliberately forget[ting] that long ago by God's Word the heavens existed and the earth was formed out of water and with water. By water also the world of that time was deluged and destroyed" (verses 5-6). The point is certain.

However, and this is our **second** point, Peter explains that God takes no pleasure in the death of the wicked (Ezekiel 33:11). He is, according to the passage, "not wanting anyone to perish, but everyone to come to repentance" (verse 9). If the wicked forget that God will bring judgment, how quickly and deliberately do we, we who call ourselves righteous, forget the terrible nature of His judgment? The prophets of the Old Testament had visions of God's judgment on the wicked, and they were terrorized by what they saw (Habakkuk 3:8-16, Daniel 8:26-27). We asked why God does not put an end to evil on His earth, but Peter responds with a challenge—we are not seeing things from God's perspective.

Third and finally, Peter reorients our thoughts by turning the view to God's experience. Paired with his deep love for His creation, God also has a unique capacity to endure.

To God, a day is like a thousand years. In "God years," it has been 730 million years since

Jesus died to bring redemption—patience is second nature to Him.

Yet to God a thousand years are like a day. If Jesus rose again on a spring Sunday morning nearly 2000 years ago, it is only Tuesday in God's calendar.

Let's never forget: God feels no rush to destroy His creatures, those for whom He has paid such a great redemption price.

Let us hear, then, this passage turned onto us. Let us see that, in this passage, Peter offers his warning to his readers—to you and me.

"[God] is patient," yes, but, "he is patient with *you*" (verse 9). He is patient with you and me even though we are impatient with Him. We cry out, "God, where is your judgment?" but Peter responds with the boldest of claims: God delays His destruction in order to see more of the wicked saved.

We accept this. But what does it mean for Peter to say we must also "speed [the day of his] coming"?

It means today is the day for us to change our perception. Today is the day to give up our grudges and hatred toward the wicked, and instead to see them with God's outreaching heart of compassion.

8
5

Forgiving:
It's Not About Me

P. Griffith Lindell, Dean,
Hoff School of Business
Corban University

Today's Reading: Psalm 32

Today's Key Verse: "Be kind and compassionate to one another, forgiving each other, just as in Christ God forgave you" (Ephesians 4:32 NIV).

Today's Insights: Forgiveness is a big topic because the biblical perspective is so very different from the culture's teaching. Western culture says: "Don't let anyone take advantage of you. Don't be too nice or too forgiving, or you will have people walk all over you."

The Bible paints a different picture.

Today's verse focuses on what Jesus Christ did for us. Our struggles with life are large to us, but to put our lives in the right perspective, we must understand that the Lord's journey to become man and live life in this world as man, yet without sin, was far, far harder on Jesus

130

than any journey any one of us will ever take no matter how great the hurt laid on us. God has forgiven those who trust in what Jesus did to save them. Therefore, the Bible says that we are always to forgive. We are always to forgive first: when, rebuffed, we are to forgive again. Why? Because God in Christ forgave us. Our gratefulness for what Jesus Christ did should be larger than any hurt we have to forgive.

I admit: this is not an easy journey. It is not in us to forgive, naturally. If we are "hurt" we want to hurt back, because we think it is all about us. If we are made angry because of what someone has done or said, we give in to anger. If we are unable to forget something in our past, it is all about us.

When it is all about us, we not only struggle with forgiving others, we also struggle with forgiving ourselves. Many reconciliations have broken down because both parties have come prepared to forgive and unprepared to be forgiven. Some people spend a lifetime trying to punish themselves for their sins instead of standing on the promises of forgiveness— because trying to punish ourselves is all about us.

Remember the story written by Edgar Allan Poe called *Tell-tale Heart*? The story is about a murderer who buries his victim in his basement, and then, filled with guilt, begins to hear what he thinks is his victim's beating heart. The heartbeats grow louder and louder (in this character's mind) until he is driven mad. The pounding heartbeat was not his victim's but his own. So it is with us when we don't forgive ourselves and others.

The excellence of Jesus Christ does not permit our flaws to be made known to the Father. He accomplishes our forgiveness. Another story may help illustrate. A wealthy man, who owned a Rolls Royce, drove it and maintained it for many years. One day, the car hit a huge pothole resulting in a broken rear axle. The owner shipped the car back to the Rolls plant in England and was surprised by the quick repair and rapid return of his car. Knowing that his warranty had run out, he kept waiting and waiting for his bill. Finally he called the factory inquiring about his bill and the reply came, "We have thoroughly searched our files and find no record of a Rolls Royce axle ever breaking." The integrity and excellence of that company would not permit a flaw in workmanship or material to be made known.

God sees us with "no record" because we have accepted his forgiveness of our sin by faith in what Jesus has done on the cross. Despite that promise, it is not in humans to easily forgive others or ourselves: that fact alone is something we must humbly admit to God, and let Him work in our hearts knowing that He will "forgive us our sins, just as we have forgiven those who have sinned against us."

Remember, the promise of God *to forgive* is about Him, not us. It is never about us; it is always about others. Philippians 2:3b says: "*Do nothing from selfishness or empty conceit,* ***but with humility of mind regard one another as more important than yourselves.***"

Forgive—because you have been forgiven.

36

Trust

Sheldon C. Nord, President
Corban University

Today's Reading: Jeremiah 17:5-18

Today's Key Verse: "Those who know your name trust in you, for you, LORD, have never forsaken those who seek you" (Psalm 9:10 ESV).

Today's Insights: Trust is a multilayered thing. When it comes to trusting an object, we do it all the time without thinking about it.

Sitting down hard in your desk chair or favorite kitchen stool? You trust those four legs. Opening a new packaged food with an unbroken seal? You trust that what's inside is fresh, clean and edible.

Driving our cars? Unless the check engine light is on or it's making funny noises, we trust without a second thought that the car will run well and get us from Point A to Point B.

When it comes to trusting another human being, trust gets complicated. We have

numerous mental filters we pass the person
through.

We ask, usually without consciously realizing
it: How long have I known him? Has he been
reliable in the past? How does he treat other
people? What is his reputation? Is he sincere in
his dealings with others, or do I sense impure
motives?

A host of other questions pass through us when
we're assessing whether to place our trust in
someone.

Then there's trust in the Lord. I don't mean the
Big Trust—the moment we choose to dedicate
our lives to Jesus Christ. For those who are
Christians already, I am referring to the many
countless times a day that we have to decide
whether or not we will trust Him.

We ask ourselves even more questions than we
do when considering whether to trust another
person. "Does He actually care about this
matter in my life?" "What if He wants
something different for me than what I want?"
And sometimes we never move to the point of
trusting Him in our circumstances because we
get caught up in our questions and stay there,
stuck.

As verse 5 in our reading shows us, we can
choose to trust in man, and draw "strength

from mere flesh." This sounds innocent enough, and even healthy to be encouraged and strengthened by our community.

But when we go to others to meet our needs and our hearts are no longer set on Jesus, the Scriptures tells us we are "cursed." That is a big deal. The process of getting to that point can happen so gradually that we don't even notice our eyes losing focus on the Lord.

On the other hand, our reading shows us that those who trust in the Lord, "whose confidence is in him," are blessed. That is just as weighty as being cursed, but on the other end of the spectrum.

Our reading then compares the blessed, trusting person with a tree planted by water. Because its roots are connected to its life source, it remains healthy and strong even in the face of inclement weather.

It "bears fruit" continually, which in a human sense, according to Galatians 5:22-23, means we are filled with love, joy, peace, patience, kindness, goodness, faithfulness, gentleness and self-control.

Trusting the Lord is not easy, and our reading acknowledges that. We will have skeptics, and our culture, taunting us and tempting us with reasons to doubt. And, because our hearts are impure (verse 9), if we default to our fickle feelings we will easily be led astray ... back to a place of doubting the Lord, His provision and His deep, rich love for us.

What, then, is our solution?

Trust. Trust is both what we strive for (our destination) and trust is also how we get there (the path leading to the destination). Learning how to trust takes practice. And practice takes discipline.

It's easy to trust when we feel it in our hearts, but it's another practice all together to choose to trust when we do not feel it. Yet we must discipline ourselves to do so, in every challenge we face. After all, the "blessing" of our souls is at stake!

37

God's Synergy, Our Good

Nancy Marshall, Director of Human Resources, Corban University

Today's Reading: Romans 8:24-39

Today's Key Verse: "And we know that for those who love God all things work together for good, for those who are called according to his purpose" (Romans 8:28 ESV).

Today's Insights: I love that the phrase "work together" comes from the Greek word *sunergon*. It's the same word from which we get "synergy," which is "the interaction of elements that when combined produce a total effect that is greater than the sum of the individual elements, contributions, etc."

I first gained experiential knowledge of the power of synergy when I found myself the unlikely focus on center stage of Madison Square Garden in 1973. I was competing in a historic gymnastics meet between the United States and China. The Chinese athletes had not competed internationally since the 1950s, and it was the first time they had visited the U.S. since the Cultural Revolution began.

As the top-ranked Olympian competing that night I had set out to win the all-around competition. But after embarrassing falls from the balance beam and uneven bars, I had no hope for a gold medal.

As I prepared for the floor exercise event, I thought, "At least I can redeem my reputation by doing well on this routine." But as I waited for my music to begin, all I heard through the speakers was garbled noise. I moved off the mat, looking to my coach for an explanation.

She cued me again. I went back to the mat only to hear the same muffled sounds. A knot tightened in my stomach. I already blew my other routines! Now this! I wanted to crawl under the mat and hide. I dreaded the prospect of performing with no music. That would like eating dry toast—boring and flavorless.

After my third attempt at a "do-over," it was clear I would not be dancing to *2001: A Space Odyssey*. And there in the middle of **Madison Square Garden** in front of **thousands of pairs of eyes**, I lost hope.

But in one of those serendipitous moments, through an interpreter, the Chinese piano player offered to help. He had never seen my routine or heard my music, but he was skilled enough to know he could improvise as I danced. And so the duet began.

We performed an unprecedented international collaboration. When all seemed hopeless, the *sunergon* took over and what transpired was far more memorable than any gold medal performance I could have ever accomplished. I finished and the audience was standing and clapping thunderously. It was a victory—for me, for Mr. Jhou, and for both of our countries.

This story is a vivid picture of synergy at its best. Who would have thought a 15-year-old girl from Urbana, Illinois and a humble pianist from Beijing could transform a broken tape into a historic demonstration of international goodwill? And all in the middle of the Cold War.

This takes me back to Romans 8:28. Perhaps you have pain, loss, heartache and unfulfilled dreams that have crashed into a ball of twisted confusion in your life. You feel defeated. Hope is a hard commodity to come by. These challenges, when viewed in isolation, make no sense at all.

But something happens when we place our circumstances in the hands of the Master Craftsman. Paul tells us they are actually working together to produce something good that is far more than we could ever ask or imagine. It's not that we suddenly understand everything, but that God—in His unique and awesome ways—produces a synergy so totally outside of our control that a brand-new outcome is formed.

Obtaining this synergy is not a process that can be rushed or forced. Things may happen instantaneously, as they did for me when the Chinese pianist volunteered to step in, or they may take years and years of having to faithfully, persistently place our unanswered questions at the Lord's feet.

The timing is, just like the synergy, beyond our control. Yet through the process our heavenly Father grows and refines us, indeed working all things for our good ... because He is good.

Thanks be to God!

The Most Important Leadership Quality

*Chris Vetter, Associate Provost of
Enrollment Management
Corban University*

Today's Reading: Philippians 2

Today's Key Verse: "[F]or it is God who works in you to will and to act in order to fulfill his good purpose" (Philippians 2:13 NIV).

Today's Insights: Do executive level leaders in Christian higher education and other fields of nonprofit endeavor need the same competencies as leaders in the for-profit world? Or can they get by with a somewhat shorter or different list?

I discovered some surprising answers during the course of my doctoral work at Gonzaga University.

First, the list of required competencies is *longer*, not shorter.

Second, the list of required competencies for nonprofit leaders expands on the established premise that leadership flows from who one is as a person. This means that when leadership competency is viewed in the broadest and most holistic terms, elements of the person of the leader must be taken into consideration as well.

Third, the list of required competencies adds Commitment to Mission/Purpose.

Fourth, the list ranks Commitment to Mission/Purpose as the #1 most important competency for a nonprofit leader. This competency was described as having a passion for the mission of the organization.

Passion, of course, is not a skill or knowledge; it flows from the values and perspective of the individual. Passion and commitment are rooted in the person of the leader.

The addition of Commitment to Mission/Purpose, and its rank as the #1 most important competency, highlights a substantive point of departure from for-profit competency models. It had a weight score of 742 over against 586 and 462 for the #2 and #3 competencies. In other words, it stands head and shoulders above all other competencies.

No executive can be expected to possess every competency, but every nonprofit leader must have a strong passion for the organization's mission and purpose. In light of the challenges he or she will face, it is critical for success.

One lens through which to view this is the out-working of a Christ-like servant leader attitude. It is impossible to imagine that Jesus Christ might have lacked passion. Rather, His passion is seen on every page of the Gospels.

No wonder the apostle Paul can say, in today's key verse, that "it is God who works in you to will and to act in order to fulfill his good purpose."

Granted, not everyone can work for a Christ-centered nonprofit, but all of us can pray, promote, have passion for and financially support such ministries. We also can bring a Christ-centered perspective and passion to the place where God has called us to serve. We all have a part to play in Kingdom building and can use our God-given talents and abilities to accomplish His purposes.

Down through the decades, Corban's mission has been and continues to be "To educate Christians who will make a difference in the world for Jesus Christ."

What's your passion?

39

The Weight of Waiting

Matt Lucas, Provost/
Executive Vice President
Corban University

Today's Reading: Psalm 27:14; 37:7, 9, 14

Today's Key Verse: "The time that the people of Israel lived in Egypt was 430 years. At the end of 430 years, on that very day, all the hosts of the LORD went out from the land of Egypt" (Exodus 12:40-41 ESV).

Today's Insights: Imagine waiting to the last day after 430 years. The Bible is full of these passages and, if you are caught up in the story itself, you can quickly pass over them: Noah's 100 years building the ark, Abraham and Sarah's lifetime wait for a child, Jacob's 20 years of work for Laban, Joseph's 10 to 12 years in prison, Israelites' 40 years of wandering, David's 4 years in Ziklag, Elijah's 22-year endurance of Ahab, and Judah's 70 years of Babylonian captivity.

In half a breath, the stories dispense with years, decades, even lifetimes. It is easy to ignore them because a handful of words impede us from the action, but when we slow down and linger over the words, they make us feel uncomfortable.

So much happens during those phrases: births, celebrations, memorable experiences, passing seasons, new acquaintances, natural disasters, lingering sicknesses, and deaths.

And while the years fly by, the accumulation of minutes, hours, days, months and years weigh us down as we wait on the Lord who sees a thousand years as a day.

If we are honest, we begin to wonder ...

- what day 125,617 felt like for Noah. Was he fashioning another tool he knew would give out before he finished?

- how Abraham and Sarah spent their 84th anniversary. Did it end in an argument because of her infertility?

- what the 12th new year festival felt like in Laban's tent. Did Jacob have to grit his teeth at another of Laban's jokes at his expense?

- what the rainy season was like for Joseph in a cold cell. Was he sick with the flu?

- what meal 10,321 of manna tasted like: How many children had known only manna as a staple?

- what the third spring looked like from the walls of Ziklag: Was David looking for a messenger from home?

- where Elijah was when Ahab married Jezebel. Was he worried about what this would mean for him?

- how the Israelites felt when they gathered for the 35th Passover in captivity. Were they having trouble finding the ingredients for the dinner?

We celebrate these men and women because of their faithfulness, but forget that their faith wasn't developed in the space of a sentence.

Instead, it was forged in the tedium of the ordinary and regular rhythm of life that did more to shape their faith than the great moments of action for which God was preparing them.

They had learned how to wait on God in the midst of what seemed like endless deferment, and how to trust in His promises while experiencing the mundane. They learned so that when great moments of their life came, they were ready to respond.

It is in waiting that our wills learn to submit to God's sovereignty and faithfulness, that our desires are brought into conformity with God's, that our character is refined.

How long are you willing to wait?

40

Holding Fast in a Frenetically Fast- Paced World

Sam Baker, Associate Professor of Ministries, Corban University

Today's Reading: Hebrews 10:22-25

Today's Key Verse: "Let us hold fast the confession of our hope without wavering, for He who promised is faithful" (Hebrews 10:23 NASB).

Today's Insights: American culture is changing on average every 5 to 7 years, at "break-neck" speed, if you will.

Take technology: When I was in high school we used to listen to music engraved on 12-inch plastic discs called "records." Remember those? You couldn't listen to records in the car, however, because you were restricted to AM-FM radio.

Soon the world experienced an invention that would allow people to listen to music both in their homes and in their cars—the 8-track! The only problem with 8-tracks was that in order to listen to your *one* favorite song, you had to listen to the entire album to return to that one song—no rewind capabilities.

Inventors, however, solved this problem by making a smaller version of magnetically-taped music in the form of the cassette tape. Now you could not only fast-forward and rewind your music, but listen to your favorite "mix tapes."

As things continued to advance, portability seemed to be the new wave of technology as compact discs (CDs) emerged on the scene. CDs resembled a small record, but were now "digitally" produced and could store 10 times more music than could be produced on a record.

Today, music is delivered in "high definition" digital formats via handheld devices that are no larger than a credit card. These devices can hold up to hundreds of thousands of songs. And if you forget how to use your device, just ask any middle-school kid; they'd be more than willing to give you a quick tutorial.

In a frenetically-paced, break-neck speed world, it's easy to get caught in the middle of all the changes, not noticing that somehow we've been impacted by it all. But let's be clear— because the Bible makes it very clear—there are some things that should *never* change.

One of the great challenges for believers today is navigating all the changes taking place around us while steadfastly hanging onto the truth we profess as believers in Jesus Christ. Verse 23 of Hebrews 10 tells us to "hold fast."

The word picture here is descriptive of someone clinging to something, in almost absolute desperation, without letting go. Take rock-climbers, for example. They refer to this as a "Thank God!" hold; getting to a point in your climb when you are able to jam your entire fist into a crack in the rock, knowing you could support your entire weight just by that one hold alone.

But to what are we holding fast? The author of Hebrews talks about "the confession of our hope" (verse 23). This verse, the preceding verse, and the verse that follows include the famous New Testament trio of "faith," "hope," and "love," but here focus specifically on "hope." And notice the emphasis on "our" hope. Our hope is a shared hope. We are the people of God, designed for community and relationship. This verse reminds us that we need each other!

Yet this verse also reminds us—as we adapt, change, and adjust—that we're not to be "tossed here and there by waves and carried about by every wind of doctrine, by the trickery of men, by craftiness in deceitful scheming"

(Ephesians 4:14). We are an unwavering people! We hold fast to the universal and unchanging truth of our faith. There is a renewed sense of calling to hold fast to the things we know to be true.

Let's get practical for a moment regarding the hectic pace of our lives, and all the distractions therein.

How have you been doing in respect to spending time in God's Word in comparison to TV watching, Facebook posting, Instagraming, Hulu binging, Googling, podcasting, emailing, texting, etc.?

Do you think you do a better job at Bible reading and praying than most pastors? A few years ago, the Francis A. Schaeffer Institute of Church Leadership Development reported the following: "72% of the pastors … only studied the Bible when they were preparing for sermons or lessons." They also reported only 26% of pastors said they regularly had personal devotions and felt they were adequately fed spirituality.[5]

I know pastors are busy and struggle with priorities. I know professors struggle. My hunch is *you* struggle too!

---

[5] Richard J. Krejcir. "Statistics on Pastors." *Into Thy Word.* http://www.intothyword.org/apps/articles/default.asp?article id=36562.

The determined effort of holding "fast to our confession of hope without wavering" becomes imperative when we spend disciplined amounts of time in God's Word and prayer, aligning ourselves with the very truths we hope to claim and defend!

And if we're faithful in this regard, get this: "He who promised is faithful." It is God who has given us the ability to have faith in the first place (verse 22). It is God who provides and maintains our hope (verse 23). It is God who helps us live out the reality of our life in Christ with others (verse 24). So how much more do you think the Lord will follow through on His promise to sustain and continue our hope until the day He returns (verse 25)?

Be reminded this day God follows through on what He says He will do, period! God makes good on His word, period! All the time, period! Now that's something I can hold onto, hope in, and believe in without wavering!

41

The Secret to "Success"

*Kevin Brubaker, Vice President for
Business, Corban University*

Today's Reading: Isaiah 6:8-13; Jonah 1:1-3

Today's Key Verse: "Now it is required that
those who have been given a trust must prove
faithful" (1 Corinthians 4:2 NIV).

Today's Insights: Two different men, two
different calls, two very different results.

When Isaiah saw a vision of the Lord on His
throne, he heard Him say, "Who will go for
us?" His reply was, "Here am I, send me!"

When the Lord called Jonah to go to the
Ninevites, he bolted for Tarsus on a ship, trying
to escape. Ultimately, God brought Jonah back
via a fish, called him again and he obeyed,
though he still didn't like it.

Who had better results in their ministry? Right
from the start, God told Isaiah what the results
of his obedience would be and it didn't look
good. Nobody would hear, nobody would
believe. Many today would call that "failure."

In contrast, Jonah had some of the most amazing results ever—an entire pagan city repented and followed the Lord. We'd call that "success."

So what gives? One man is willing and had no results and the other obeyed kicking and screaming and had great results. In today's world, Jonah would sign a book deal and write about how to lead pagan cities to repentance. Jonah did write a book, perhaps in reflection later in life, showing how God used a less than willing messenger to accomplish His perfect will. Jonah depicted himself as a reluctant participant in God's great plan.

Isaiah also wrote a book and chronicled God's judgment and His mercy. His eloquent prophecy of the coming Servant and Savior of all has often been titled the "First Gospel." Yet, if you would have asked Isaiah if he was a success, I think all he could have said was, "I was obedient to the Lord."

Today, we think of Isaiah as the greater servant because he followed the Lord with his whole heart. But if we would have looked at the two prophets back then, we would have praised Jonah because of the great revival of Nineveh.

My point is this: be careful how you judge the results of someone's ministry, and always be sure to give God the praise rather than His servants. If God can create a great revival using a rebellious prophet who never wanted to see his audience repent, how highly should I think of myself when my ministry flourishes? Was it really about me? Should I write a book about my methods?

On the other hand, I might think that there is zero success for my faithful efforts but fail to realize that God is doing something I could never imagine and will never see in my lifetime.

My task is to be a faithful, obedient servant and let God do the rest, giving him the glory at all times. This is something I could do better. How about you?

42

How Do I Know God Loves Me When Things Are Bad?

Gary Derickson, Professor of Biblical Studies, Corban University

Today's Reading: Romans 5:8

Today's Key Verse: "But God demonstrates His own love toward us, in that while we were still sinners, Christ died for us" (NKJV).

Today's Insights: God did not send His Son in order to show us His love. He sent His Son *because* He loves us. We recognize His love by His act of sending. God's motive for sending Jesus was His love for us, not a desire to show us that He is loving.

How do I know God really loves me? As I look at myself and see my sin and how often I fail God as well as others, how can I be sure God really loves me? This question plagued me for years though I had been a child of God from childhood. I had grown up hearing this verse preached and taught, always with a focus on God wanting to prove His love for us.

Then, one day the truth of what Paul was saying struck home. It was *while* we were still sinners, *while* we were not meeting any divine standard of acceptability, God acted. He acted before I responded.

Then a second truth struck home. It was not because God was showing me or anybody else His love. Rather, God's action made His love recognizable to me. I know He loves me because of what He did.

As Paul tells us in Romans 8:31-39, because God "did not spare His own Son" we can know that nothing in the universe can separate us from His love for us. Assurance comes from understanding the full significance of God's deep, priceless, all-giving love for each of us.

This reality should guide us when we face trials and tragedy. We know God is sovereign in our lives and so it has to be allowed by God. And, He reminds us in His word that we can trust Him *because* He gave His Son.

James tells us to rejoice ("consider it joy") when we face trials. Why? In the context of James' command, he states the truth that only good gifts come from God. Therefore, that trial or tragedy is ultimately for *my* good, not just God's or someone else's. I must believe that. However, I cannot unless I really trust God. John reminds us that God's love, when brought to its complete expression in us ("perfected"), casts out fear (1 John 4:18). He is speaking in terms of our fear of judgment when we stand before Jesus at the end of our lives.

However, the same principle is true when facing the trials of James' epistle. As we walk with the Lord, we see these events as designed by God for *our* good.

For that matter, even God's discipline (Hebrews 12:3-11) is a loving action on His part, an action we are to respond to appropriately. When we do, we grow and experience the blessings of His desires for us. However, I cannot respond in faith, with joy, in submission to His will, unless I believe it is an expression of His love for me.

I must go back to the cross and remember that God's love for each of us is eternally seen in the gift of His Son.

God does not leave us with just that one demonstration of His love. He acts on our behalf in answered prayer, when we are obedient, and discipline, when we are not. His involvement in our lives is no less motivated by love when we are disobedient than when we obey. It's just different. In both cases He may take us through trials to make us more like His Son.

What will be different is that in one case He is removing something (discipline) and in the other adding (growth). He is usually doing both at once. I have experienced this more than once in my life. What follows is just one example.

In answer to God's call to the ministry, I resigned my Army commission and went off to seminary. I was in the center of God's will and knew it. However, I needed to learn more than the seminary classroom could give me. So, by God's design, my "seminary" education began with a parasite.

Two weeks before leaving to take first-year Greek in a nine-week summer course, I drank some hot tea at a restaurant on the North Rim of the Grand Canyon. The water had Giardia. I became nauseated day and night. I had an allergic reaction (seizures) and nearly died from the medication for nausea given me by my doctor.

After repeated medical tests I was told by one of Houston's leading gastro-intestinal specialists that my condition was untreatable and I would have to get used to being nauseated for the rest of my life.

I returned to my dorm room in Dallas the next day and lay in bed thinking that I would rather die than go on living with the level of misery I was experiencing. I had lost hope.

Before packing my bags, dropping out of school, and going home to die, I decided to go to chapel one last time. It was a divine appointment. The chapel speaker's message was about how Joseph handled his trials with integrity and faith in God. God could not have spoken more clearly if He had spoken audibly. I was to trust Him and keep going. So I did.

Had I "passed" the test and could move forward in my education, relatively nausea free? In answer to these questions, I can say that God did act quickly on my behalf. How? A day or two later I developed a one inch tear in my colon and was on a bulk laxative for the next six months. I continued to be nauseated twenty-four hours a day for the next two and a half years.

Only then, through a nurse friend who got concerned and researched the parasite that started the adventure, I learned that I was lactose intolerant. I had been drinking three glasses of milk every day and eating tons of cheese because they were "good for me." I cut out all dairy products and after three days felt better than I had in all of my life!

So why did God put me through those three years? Looking back I see I was overconfident in my ability to speak. I was self-sufficient. That self-confidence needed to be purged from my life. During those three years God stripped me of my confidence and made me dependent on Him every time I got up to speak. To this day, as I go to teach class, I very often pray, "by the strength which You supply." He has made me dependent so His power can be expressed through me.

He also added something to me. I know what it is like for someone to be told by a doctor, "You will never get better. This is the best you will ever feel again." Where in my youthful health I could not identify with the sick and dying, I am now comfortable in their presence. God has enabled me to minister to His dying children and, hopefully, be a source of encouragement and comfort.

Now, as I age I face health issues along with the other trials of life. How can I handle the challenges? How can any of us face these things with joy?

We do so by remembering that we have a God who loves us, who has always loved us, and who will always love us. We have seen His love in action. And if we just look a little closer through the lens of His love, even in the trial, we will see His love once again.

43

How Do We Use Power and Authority?

Leroy Goertzen, Associate Professor of Pastoral Theology, Corban University

Today's Reading: Philippians 2:3-11

Today's Key Verse: "Do nothing out of selfish ambition or vain conceit, but in humility consider others better than yourselves" (Philippians 2:3 NIV).

Today's Insights: The temptation to abuse power and authority is pervasive and dangerous. We are familiar with Lord Acton's famous quote: "Power tends to corrupt, and absolute power corrupts absolutely."

We don't need to look far or long to see examples of power's corruption. It exists in some form at every level and structure of society be it families, schools, churches, businesses, the military and government— to name a few.

A perusal of the latest news proves that human beings of every color and creed struggle with using power and authority responsibly.

The audience to which Paul penned this well-known passage was all too familiar with power's abuse. Philippi was a colony repopulated with expatriate Roman soldiers who reorganized the city's social and political structures after the hierarchy of the military. This created a stratified society characterized by an insatiable quest for social honor and position.

Should you have opportunity to visit ancient Philippi you would no doubt see honorific inscriptions amidst the first century archaeological remains. Pillars, foundation stones, and statues reveal extensive lists of positions and offices held by those who dedicated these various objects to the city. This incessant need to list honors is referred to as the *cursus honorum* (the courses of offices)— the sequential order of public offices held by aspiring politicians in the Roman state. It would appear that the original audience of Paul's letter reflected this way of life—one described by Paul as "selfish ambition and vain conceit" (2:3).

In today's reading, Paul demonstrates that Jesus' life necessarily took a radically different direction—one that theologians refer to as the *cursus pudorum*—the courses of ignominies. Notice that Paul describes Jesus' course of ignominies through two distinct downward movements.

First, Paul states that, even though Jesus Christ was in very nature God, He did not take advantage or exploit that position (2:6). Frank Thielman writes in his commentary on Philippians: "His (Christ's) equality with God led him to view his status not as a matter of privilege but as a matter of unselfish giving."

Jesus demonstrated this attitude in a concrete way by taking action; "making himself nothing" which he did by "taking the very nature of a servant," and "being made in human likeness." These phrases indicate that Jesus, the Son of God, became a human in every sense, but without any social advantage and with few or no rights or privileges of His own. He did this in order to dedicate Himself completely to the service of others.

Jesus testified, "For even the Son of Man did not come to be served, but to serve, and to give his life as a ransom for many" (Matthew 20:28). In taking the very nature of a servant, of a slave, Jesus elected to identify personally with those assigned to the most dishonorable public status. When Paul frames Jesus as a slave, he assigns to him a position of greatest disgrace and shame in the social world of the Philippians. This could not have been more shocking and disturbing.

In 2:8 Jesus Christ's condescension involves a second ignominy: he humbled himself by becoming obedient to death—not just any death—but the most dishonorable, humiliating one known to his world—crucifixion. Jesus has now reached the nadir of condescension—you can't stoop any lower than this. And Jesus does this exactly because He is God.

Again, Theilman writes, "Christ went from the highest position imaginable to the lowest precisely because such selfless love is an expression of his deity."

Paul concludes this section (verses 9-11) with a description of how God the Father has responded to His Son's course of ignominies and what that means. He exalts Him to the place of recognizable superiority and honor over all creation that is accompanied appropriately with a new name—a name that gives universal recognition to who Jesus has always been—Lord and God.

This text is intended to serve as an example of how believers are to live in a world consumed with prestige, power and position. It's not that these are bad in themselves. In fact, they can become the means by which good is done. We tend, however, to be self-absorbed using what influence we have to serve self-interest to the degree that the concerns and needs of others are ignored and neglected.

To the contrary, missiologist Yves Raguin

states, "By dispossessing ourselves, we are able to absorb the amazing riches of others." This is what Paul had in mind for the Philippian believers.

Jesus radically dispossessed status and privilege—the prerogatives of Deity—and willingly used His power and position of Deity for the sake of others—in the unselfish giving of Himself so that God's grace and forgiveness could be extended to all, even to those responsible for His crucifixion (Luke 23:34).

God's presence is manifest in our lives when we humbly and selflessly use what power and authority we have for the benefit of others.

44

Cathedral Dive

Pam Teschner, Associate Provost of
Academics, Corban University

Today's Reading: 1 Corinthians 2:6-13

Today's Key Verse: "The Spirit, not content to flit around on the surface, dives into the depths of God, and brings out what God planned all along" (1 Corinthians 2:10 MSG).

Today's Insights: Hovering in scuba gear on the edge of a coral reef in Lanai's tropical waters, I peered into the mysterious blue depths below. It was exactly like the drop-off scene in the movie, *Nemo*. The reef was alive with schools of beautiful angelfish, tangs, and butterfly fish creating spectacular splashes of color.

There was a moment of apprehension as I glanced up at the bottom of the boat from which I had just leaped. But the lure of the deep drew me over the edge of the reef and into the vastness below. Like Nemo, I had a few daring friends urge me on, and we all drifted weightless into the depths. We were on our way to the famous underwater cathedral.

Slowly descending, I became fascinated with a parrotfish biting off pieces of coral. I drifted over to watch and hung weightless beside him, rhythmically pulling air through the mouthpiece. Ignoring me, he continued crunching coral for the tasty morsel inside. He had obviously seen rubberized bubbling creatures before meeting me and wasn't taken aback by the out-of-world intrusion.

I kicked to catch up with the group as they approached a rock formation. Great tubes and caves had been created by hot lava spilling into the water many years in the distant past. We ventured into these tunnels and caves until finally entering a great underwater cathedral.

Sunlight from above shone through holes high up the wall creating a stained glass effect. Shafts of blue light illuminated the cave with a soft glow. I hung weightless in the open space of the cathedral enveloped by the great secret of the deep. A mysterious sense of holiness pervaded the silence.

Most people splash in the safety of the shallows, never experiencing the uncommon mysteries of the depths. Some race around tearing up the surface, exhilarated by the thrill of the ride. Some have been carried deep by the weights of the surface and discovered unimaginable treasure tucked away in unexpected places.

We were designed to venture into the mysterious depths of God, but the deep is unnerving. It strips and exposes the corruption of the soul but engulfs it with nearly unbearable peace. The broken and repentant heart finds the inestimable treasure of forgiveness and faith in the depths of holiness. But one must leap out of the boat and risk the drop-off to find the treasure.

Oh, to be in the place where God opens His heart and reveals inexpressible truth. In the quiet of holy depths, with only my breath breaking the silence, the unutterable language of the Spirit echoes in the cathedrals of my heart … *Abba, Father*!

45

Planning …

P. Griffith Lindell, Dean,
Hoff School of Business
Corban University

Today's Reading: Proverbs 16:9, 25, 33

Today's Key Verse: "We can make our plans, but the LORD determines our steps" (Proverbs 16:9 NLT).

Today's Insights: Planning is important. Sometimes, even after all the careful plans, one "throws the dice" to determine a decision since one course of action cannot be weighed effectively against another—the correct one cannot be determined.

Mintzberg & Quinn have observed that the planning process plays a key role in strategy formation and a well-structured process will provide a framework for change management. Good planning is vital to an organization's health and growth.

One quote from their work strikes me as important in the context of the verses above: "Strategy deals with the unknowable, not the uncertain." Business leaders work hard at looking at patterns, factors, trends, research, known and unknown needs—elements, among others, that go into plans; but they do not know the future. God does. When success comes from both great strategy formulation and implementation, man often takes the credit—robbing God of His holiness.

Planning and the power of foresight allows leaders to see opportunity even in a world of issues and problems to be solved. The strategy that emerges from planning is the result of the synergy between the **lessons of the past** and the **realities of the present**. These are connected in such a way that the potentials for both intended and unintended consequences in the future represent the right thinking at the right time and in the right manner.

However, for the Christian in business, it is good to remember that self-propelled plans produce death. If it is about me or the business and not about God, it is worth nothing.

Eternity matters, now. Even with planning, nothing happens anywhere without God's involvement. His sovereignty is so majestic that we don't understand how our freedom, even to commit sin, can be used by Him for His glory. Although God does not author sin, His purposes are so powerful that He allows man's rebellion to achieve His eternal paradigm.

Although planning is about the future, it is good also to remember Blaise Pascal's thought in *Pensées*: "We never keep to the present. We recall the past; we anticipate the future as if we found it too slow in coming and were trying to hurry it up, or we recall the past as if to stay its too rapid flight ... The fact is that the present usually hurts. We thrust it out of sight because it distresses us, and if we find it enjoyable, we are sorry to see it slip away. We try to give the support of the future, and think how we are going to arrange things over which we have no control for a time we can never be sure of reaching."

There is a tension in planning. Jesus challenged His audience about the importance of planning: "For which of you, desiring to build a tower, does not first sit down and count the cost, whether he has enough to complete it?" (Luke 14:28).

The Christian business leader should use good planning and management techniques to control the business: but s/he does this with the absolute certainty that the LORD determines the outcome. Because God does that, this in no way excuses people from planning, thinking, and strategizing. In fact, His Word has much to say about the strength of counselors when formulating plans.

A formula to consider is this: Plan. Pray.

Practice. Perform. Pray. Ponder (what is God saying in this performance about Himself and about my role in His kingdom?). Pray. Perform. There is a constant here: our Creator cares and His care calms our concerns when we practice prayer.

It is Jeremiah's assertion that strikes me as a life-changing realization. His life was by no means enviable from the worlds' point of view. But he understood what God called him to do—and he did it, sometimes kicking and screaming, but always with the resolute understanding that God is sovereign and loving and caring and holy.

Believers rest in the promise in Psalm 37. We must first think about what we do as "Lord-delighting-plans." And then we must marshal our people to plan—developing the discipline for our managers to look ahead and to be intentional about communicating goal progress, resource allocation and the impact of short-term plans on the vision and mission (the strategy) of the organization, remembering that strategy begins in the heart.

Planning is good. Praying is essential.

46

Power Restored

Jim Hills, Professor of Humanities
Corban University

Today's Reading: Romans 1:16-21

Today's Key Verse: "For I am not ashamed of the gospel of Christ: for it is the power of God unto salvation to everyone that believeth" (Romans 1:16 KJV).

Today's Insights: I arrived home on the first hot day of the year to find that the house was without power. My household was, the newspaper reported the next day, one of about ten thousand customers left without electricity because of a failed insulator. The paper noted that the outage knocked out traffic signals at several major intersections, creating "chaos at rush hour."

Things were fouled up at home, too. Dirty laundry lay in a heap in front of the useless washing machine. The house was getting hot, and of course the fans wouldn't work. The TV room in the basement was cool, but the television was out of commission, and without lights it was too dim down there to read. I began to worry about the food in the freezer, and my grandson and I decided we should eat the ice cream before it melted. He took the French vanilla and I finished off the butter pecan.

The computer was laid up, too. But the biggest problem was water. We live at the edge of town in a house built when this was countryside, and we get our water from a well. The electric pump was out, of course, and we began to see how important that was. The toilet tank could not refill. The morning's dirty dishes stayed dirty. And on an afternoon with temperatures in the mid-nineties, so did we. There were no showers for our hot, sticky bodies.

The main electrical failure had produced a ripple effect, the smaller stations directing power to individual neighborhoods going down like dominos. But the men in hard hats worked on into the warm night, and finally power and order were restored. This morning the washing machine is humming as the pile of dirty laundry shrinks. There's ice in the freezer and cool milk in the fridge. At the touch of a button I fill the house with music.

I've had a hot breakfast of soft-boiled eggs on toast with three slices of bacon cooked crisp in the microwave. And best of all, I'm clean—yesterday's sweat and fret sluiced down the drain by a rush of hot, healing water. It is, as Mr. Rogers liked to say, a beautiful day in the neighborhood.

I've been reminded about what happens when the electron flow that does so much to make our lives clean, comfortable, and productive is interrupted; about the chaos, misery, and difficulty of lives without power; about what happens, for instance, when not just electrical lines but human beings short out; about what happened in Eden when there occurred a catastrophic spiritual power outage and the line between the Creator and the creatures came down; about the sweat and dirt and disease that followed; about the chaos of a world "off-line," and all the painful effects of the original and massive power outage.

I've been reminded, too, that if I meant to restore my home to order there was only one way to do it: I had to have the power back. There was just no other way, no other plan, no other process. I had to get reconnected.

Every drill sergeant barking orders knows, better than the boys, why they must endure the hard things he makes them do. They have a great commission, a noble duty, and they must be connected and strengthened in order to do it.

Scripture reminds us that our Great Captain was tested in every way that we are. He knew hunger and thirst, knew the hatred of those who opposed Him, knew the sting of betrayal.

His life was difficult. Yet He was so strong a tomb could not keep Him.

Scripture tells us we are in conflict with a powerful and cunning adversary. "Did we in our own strength confide," Martin Luther wrote, "our striving would be losing," a caution to keep in mind when we encounter the testings that will make us strong.

We do well to think about the One who said, "All power is given unto me" and the ways He intends to direct that power through every believer to bring light to a darkened world, warmth to cold hearts, living water to thirsty souls. For the gospel, after all, is "the power of God unto salvation to everyone that believeth."

47

"Do You Believe In Miracles?"

Marty Trammell, Chair of Humanities
Corban University

Today's Reading: Genesis 17:1-22

Today's Key Verse: "Then Abraham fell on his face and laughed, and said in his heart, 'Will a child be born to a man one hundred years old? And will Sarah, who is ninety years old, bear a child?'" (Genesis 17:17 NASB).

Today's Insights: "Do you believe in miracles?" Al Michael's voice turned that question into a dramatic statement as the U.S. Hockey team defeated the Soviets in the 1980 Olympic games.

Known as the "miracle on ice" the game lives on as *Sports Illustrated's* "Top Sports Moment of the 20th Century."

Do you believe in miracles? Abraham and Sarah must have asked themselves that question often as the years passed through empty weeks and anxious days.

Twenty-five years after the promise (Genesis 12), Abraham and Sarah still woke up every morning without the son of promise, still strangers in the land promised to them a quarter of a century earlier. It's difficult to believe the impossible when you don't see God at work every day.

Like Sarah, Mary had to believe the impossible. She must have asked herself a hundred times, "God will become a man and be born as a baby, a baby I will give birth to and raise?" But God created miracles, and in some senses, He can do nothing less.

All His works are miracles if we stop and think about them. The miracle of life in Sarah's womb. The miracle of love in Mary's. The miracles of forgiveness, restoration and friendship with the One who made us. These last three are just as real as the ones recorded in the biblical text, but we find so much to question in them. Sometimes God changes these questions into dramatic statements, too.

The March 3, 1980 issue of *Sports Illustrated* has no other words on its cover. Only the picture of the Olympic hockey team celebrating the "miracle on ice." Hans Kluetmeier, the photographer, said the picture "didn't need any words." Maybe he's right.

Maybe miracles need few words because they

live more dramatically in the pictures God creates in our lives. The miracle of Isaac, the son of promise, and the miracle of Jesus, the promised Son, and the miracles of our relationship with God are pictured so clearly in the lives of ordinary people. Ordinary people who, even in the cold arenas of our routines, experience the extraordinary.

Everyday life can be about letting the people around us see the front page picture of God forgiving our sins, transforming our weaknesses—and keeping His promises in you and me.

So Al Michaels was right, it's not a question; it's a dramatic statement: "Do you believe in miracles!"

48

"Everything Is Awesome"

Kristin Dixon, Dean,
School of Education and Counseling
Corban University

Today's Reading: Psalm 40, Psalm 86:10, Psalm 139:14

Today's Key Verse: "For you are great and do marvelous deeds; you alone are God" (Psalm 86:10 NIV).

Today's Insights: The title for today's devotion may cause you to hum a particular tune from the Lego movie.

We live in a culture where—it seems—most everything is awesome or amazing, so much so that the meaning and emphasis of those words have been diluted.

The Scriptures for today's reading have one common concept or word (depending on which version one is reading) that is not as overused in popular language as awesome and amazing, but which speaks to the awe and amazement we might and should feel when considering God's attributes, character, and works of sacrificial love, mercy, and grace.

Consider the concept and meaning behind the words marvelous and marvel. Marvel is from the Latin word *mirari*, which means to wonder at. Used as a verb, marvel allows us to be filled with wonder at God's many works. Marvelous is defined as causing great wonder; other synonyms for marvelous include extraordinary, spectacular, remarkable, magnificent and glorious, to name just a few. Marveling is defined as being filled with wonder or astonishment.

Surely, God is worthy of our marveling—or being filled with wonder and astonishment—and so are the works of the Lord.

In Psalm 40, we are told "LORD, my God, You have done great things: **marvelous** works and your thoughts toward us. There is no one who compares to you! I will try to recite your actions, even though there are too many to number."

The writer tells us that God's works and thoughts are marvelous, so much so that nothing and no one compares to God. Even an attempt to recite God's actions falls short as they are innumerable or beyond one's ability to count.

In Psalm 86:10, we are given this reminder: "For you are great and do **marvelous** deeds; you alone are God." Again, we have the opportunity to be astonished over the incomparable deeds and greatness of God.

In our daily lives, how often do we stop to marvel or to be in awe or to be amazed? A look up to the sky could cause wonder at a sunset or sunrise, at the formation of the clouds, or the power of a thunderstorm. Perhaps the views of a mountain or the ocean could cause us to acknowledge the majesty of our Creator.

How often do we marvel at God's grace and mercy in our lives—mercy so great that He sent His only son as a sacrifice for our sin? Can we marvel at the sovereignty of God who knows us?

Finally, we can marvel over these words from Psalm 139:14 KJV: "I will praise thee; for I am fearfully and wonderfully made: **marvelous** are thy works; and that my soul knoweth right well."

The process of marveling upon God's works should cause us to praise the Lord. There seems to be no other appropriate response besides praise and adoration for a God who inspires awe, whose grace is amazing, and whose very nature causes us to be filled with wonder and astonishment. Truly, these are words over which we can marvel!

49

Committed to Excellence

Sheldon C. Nord, President
Corban University

Today's Reading: Genesis 1

Today's Key Verse: "Whatever you do, work at it with all your heart, as working for the Lord, not for human masters, since you know that you will receive an inheritance from the Lord as a reward. It is the Lord Christ you are serving" (Colossians 3:23-24 NIV).

Today's Insights: Have you ever had a great shopping experience? One that leaves you not only happy with your purchase, but satisfied by the memory of the entire experience? This, I am convinced, is due to the business's commitment to exceptional customer service.

We have a tire store where I live that goes above and beyond the call of duty. The employees are knowledgeable, friendly, and intent on making sure you walk away impressed. And you do. Every time! Their policies are customer-centric (bought chains years ago, but never used them? Return them

185

and get fully refunded), and their employees are eager to serve (they literally run up to the counter to assist you, or back to your vehicle to check on it). Their business model is working, and working well.

I also know of a particular department store that shines in the area of customer service. Employees go the extra mile to ensure the customer gets exactly what he or she is looking for, even if they have to obtain a different size or color from another store. This store has countless loyal customers, and many are happy to pay more just for the service.

Now think about a negative shopping experience. You may have eventually walked away with the item you wanted, but the experience was so bad that you've made up your mind to never return.

Consider this: did either experience happen at companies that were specifically "Christian" or "secular"? I am certain there is no distinction; poor and outstanding customer service happen wherever we go.

At Corban University, I am determined to see our quality of service shine. I certainly don't want to be outdone by a "secular" tire or department store. Every one of our staff and faculty members signs a statement of faith, so we are all committed to serving the same God.

And our God is a God of excellence. The work of His hands, as we see from our reading, He declares "very good." We also know that we are made in His image (verses 26-27). As such, I believe the work of our hands—whatever it is God has called us to do—is to be excellent, just as the creation story in Genesis 1 shows us (along with nature's testimony) that the work of the Lord's hands is exceptional.

I know all too well that it's not easy to be "on" all the time. We are human and we tire easily. We forget things. We become irritable. But as our verse of the day reminds us, *where* we fix our eyes has everything to do with the heart and attitude we will have as we go about our work.

Are we looking for approval from our peers or our boss? Surely discouragement will come. But when we focus on Jesus Christ, and as we contemplate the manner in which He went about His work—as a carpenter, doctor, friend, teacher and minister—we see the compassion in His eyes and the mercy He so abundantly lavished on those with whom He came in contact.

This is whom we serve. He is our perfect example of excellence. And we, too, can bring excellence to our places of work, loving and serving the people in front of us day in and day out, just as Jesus did.

Your Turn!

Want to share copies of this book with family, friends, associates, members?

Please send a quick note to the author at president@corban.edu

Made in the USA
San Bernardino, CA
22 February 2016